CREATIVE
LOG CABIN
PATCHWORK

CREATIVE LOG CABIN PATCHWORK

PAULINE BROWN

Guild of Master Craftsman Publications Ltd

First published 2003 by
Guild of Master Craftsman Publications Ltd
166 High Street, Lewes
East Sussex, BN7 1XU

ISBN 1 86108 325 4

British Cataloguing in Publication Data
A catalogue record of this book is available from the British Library.

Publisher: Paul Richardson
Art Director: Ian Smith
Managing Editor: Gerrie Purcell
Production Manager: Stuart Poole
Editor: Gill Parris
Designer: John Hawkins
Photographer: Anthony Bailey
Illustrator: Penny Brown

Typeface: Meridien

Colour reproduction by Viscan Graphics Pte Ltd, Singapore

Printed and bound by Stamford Press Ltd (Singapore)

ACKNOWLEDGEMENTS

My thanks to all the patchworkers and
textile artists who have lent their work and
photographic images. These have greatly
enhanced the visual impact of this book.

CONTENTS

INTRODUCTION

Log Cabin is an age-old patchwork technique, the beauty of which lies mainly in the choice and arrangement of colour and fabrics. The basic method consists of square blocks made from a selection of strips of fabric stitched around a central square. These blocks can be joined together in different formations to create a wide variety of designs. For those who have little time to spare, Log Cabin is one of the quickest machine methods. If you prefer the slower pace of working by hand, the intricacies of its complex designs and colour combinations will give hours of pleasure.

The history of patchwork in general goes back several hundred years and involves a journey from Europe to the USA and back again. Patchwork originally developed as a thrifty but decorative way of using old fabrics to create bed covers and quilts. It became a widespread rural craft in the United Kingdom, particularly in Wales and Northern England, and examples of quilts which derive from this tradition can be seen in both local and national museums.

Left: **Pano Picante** *by Flavin Glover. A range of Log Cabin variations, machine-pieced and hand quilted*

When the original European settlers went to the East coast of America in the eighteenth century, they took with them their needlecraft skills and developed patchwork and quilting to such an extent that it became part of the American craft heritage, and it has remained popular ever since. Major quilt shows are part of this popularity and take place on a regular basis in many states.

In Europe there was a decline in the nineteenth century due to industrialization, but in the past 50 years there has been a resurgence of interest and the patterns and techniques, which those original pioneering people developed in America, have returned to great popularity.

There are a number of legends relating to the Log Cabin design. The most well known is that a red central square represents the hearth, and the surrounding strips symbolize the logs from which the cabins were made. Additionally, the contrasting diagonal patterns of these original quilts depict the way in which sunlight was cast on the cabin walls. Sometimes the centre was made in yellow, representing a welcoming light for visitors

and family alike. It is also said that, during the Civil War, Log Cabin quilts with black central squares were hung outside houses to secretly identify stops on the underground railroad. Among the traditional patterns with strongly contrasting blocks are those entitled 'Barn Raising', with its focus on a diagonal mirrored design, and 'Straight Furrow', with the blocks arranged to form diagonal stripes.

Since those early days, the craft has been extended and developed so that there are now a vast number of ways of interpreting the technique. Such is Log Cabin's versatility that the focus may be on colour, texture or form. The original square format can be adapted to include other central geometric shapes such as triangles, rectangles, hexagons or diamonds whilst the scale of the strips can vary from very narrow to wide. You can even work in a more random fashion, with the central shape and the strips cut in uneven sizes. Leftover scraps of fabrics from dressmaking or soft furnishing projects can be fashioned into coordinating accessories and, unlike some other patchwork methods, different weights and thicknesses of fabric can be used in a single article. You can also dye, print, or marble your own fabrics, use

different types of materials such as velvet or satin, create a variety of shapes and combine the blocks with other patchwork techniques, appliqué or embroidery.

Although this type of patchwork has been used mainly for quilts and throws, other household and soft furnishing articles such as cushions, curtains or tablecloths are also a possibility. Small items for kitchen, dining room or bathroom include pot-holders, tissue-box covers, table mats and runners, whilst on a larger scale wallhangings of all shapes and sizes can be created.

If you enjoy making small gifts, you can use Log Cabin for book covers, greetings-card inserts or needle cases. It is also suitable for making up into garments such as jackets and waistcoats. You can make attractive tote bags and evening purses or add borders as a decorative finish to clothes and accessories.

In its simplest form, Log Cabin is an ideal vehicle for the beginner and can be worked by hand or machine. Very little equipment is needed and with a modicum of accuracy it is quick to do. At its most complex, it can give opportunities to the talented to explore and experiment with technique, colour, fabrics and patterns.

Left: **Canterbury Fields** *by Flavin Glover.*
Rectangular Log Cabin and Crazy Patchwork,
machine pieced and hand quilted

MAKING A START

EQUIPMENT AND MATERIALS

Sewing Equipment

One of the main advantages when embarking on Log Cabin patchwork is that you can start with just a few basic tools and, if necessary, add to them as the need arises. You will already have scissors, needles, pins, etc. in your work box, and these can be supplemented with paper, pencils and rulers. A sewing machine is of course essential for machine patchwork, and also an iron for pressing the work to an immaculate finish.

Needles and Pins

The traditional needles for all types of patchwork are sharps, which are short with round eyes but, if you prefer, you can use embroidery (crewel) needles which have long eyes. They come in several sizes, the higher the number the finer the needle. Choose the size which suits your method of stitching and one which goes comfortably through the fabric. If you are going to quilt the patchwork, betweens, which are short, are the traditional choice but again, if you prefer, you can use sharps or embroidery needles.

You will need to pin the strips of fabric firmly together and pins should be fine and rust-free. Long, coloured, glass-headed pins are also useful if you are quilting the patchwork.

Scissors and Cutting Equipment

A large pair of scissors is needed for cutting out, and a smaller pair of embroidery scissors for intricate tasks and for trimming the ends of thread. You may also need a pair of medium-size scissors for cutting patterns or templates. Paper blunts the blades very easily, so it is advisable to keep

Left: **Southwold Beach Huts – Moonlight,** *by Greta Fitchett. The log cabin outer border surrounds an appliqué centre panel and inner border with colours that have been chosen to depict the subject successfully*

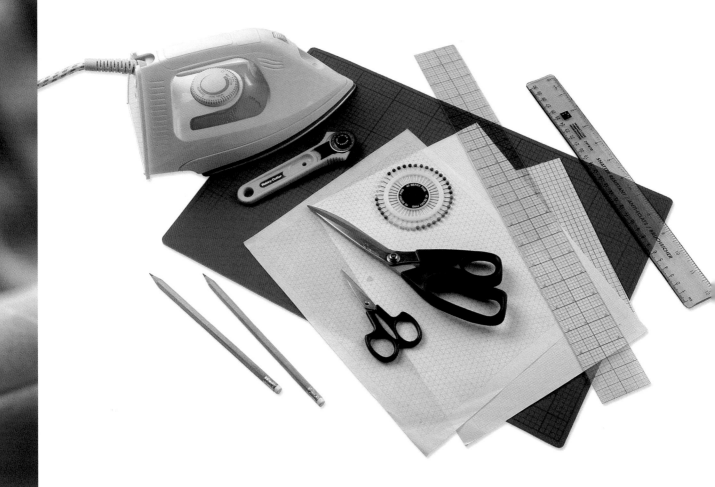

A selection of design materials and equipment

your paper scissors separate from the others, or mark them with a ribbon tie.

One of the most useful pieces of equipment for cutting the strips for Log Cabin patchwork is the rotary cutter. These are available in three sizes in both right- and left-handed versions (see 'Using a Rotary Cutter', on page 12). The blades should be changed as soon as they show signs of becoming blunt. Some shops offer a blade-sharpening service, or you can use a gadget specially made for the purpose.

A rotary cutter is used in conjunction with a wide quilter's rule and a self-healing cutting mat. Usually, these both have measurements in centimetres or inches marked on them, so it is a simple task to cut fabrics to a specific size. Those with a diagonal line or lines marked on them are useful for cutting bias strips for trimming your work. Unless you are thinking of transporting your equipment regularly to classes or a quilting group, it is advisable to choose the largest cutting mat you can afford, together with a quilter's rule long enough to extend the full width of the mat.

Although these items may seem expensive, they are worthwhile investments. Not only do they enable you to cut strips for Log Cabin with accuracy and ease, but they also speed up the process for bindings, pipings and frills, and all the other patchwork techniques.

Specialist Patchwork Accessories

Besides the rotary cutter, self-healing mat and wide quilter's rule, there are a number of other rulers made specifically as pattern guides for some variations of Log Cabin – such as the pineapple pattern – which will help you to cut fabric at the appropriate width and assemble the strips correctly. These can be purchased as the need arises.

A quarter seamer is helpful for marking 6mm (¼in) seam allowances. This usually takes the form of a square-section plastic rod which you use as a narrow ruler. A large cork mat or square of soft- or foam-board is ideal for pinning out prepared blocks before assembling them.

Fabric Markers

There are a number of specialist fabric markers on the market, but for the purposes of Log Cabin, you will only need a quilter's lead pencil or an ordinary HB or B pencil, sharpened to a point, for marking the cutting lines on fabric if you are not in possession of a rotary cutter and mat.

If you intend to finish your project with decorative quilting or embroidery designs, the fabric should be marked lightly with a dotted line as this will be unlikely to show when the stitching is complete. There are several markers which are suitable on these occasions.

A water-erasable pen (see overleaf)

Silver and soapstone markers are useful for items which will eventually be laundered as they will wash out with soap and water. The marks made with blue water-erasable pens will also disappear with the application of water, but you should not iron the fabric before doing this as the heat may set the ink.

If you are using silk or rayon fabrics, test the marker to ensure that water marks are not left when the design is erased. Air-erasable pens, with their fine purple lines, stay visible for up to twelve hours, so are only suitable for small short-term projects.

Doubts have been expressed regarding the long-term effects which air- and water-erasable markers have on fabric fibres, so it may be advisable not to use them on items which you intend to be the heirlooms of the future, or for commissions for hangings or quilts.

Sewing Machines

The sophisticated nature of modern sewing machines, with their automatic and computerized stitches and various attachments for a wide variety of uses, makes them exciting to use. They are, however, not essential for making up Log Cabin articles or for machine quilting. A standard electric machine with a few basic attachments is all that is necessary. A walking (or quilting foot) will ride smoothly over wadding and several layers of fabric and a zipper foot is essential for zips and piping. A machine which enables you to alter the needle position is useful for setting the width of the seam allowance and you will need to be able to disengage the feed for free-machining (see page 87).

Quilting Accessories

If you intend to quilt your Log Cabin project, you will need a quilting frame, such as a hoop, a tubular frame, or a traditional rectangular tapestry or quilting frame (see page 84). These are all available in several sizes so can be chosen to suit your particular needs.

Many people feel that the use of a thimble is a matter of choice, but when quilting you will probably find that the protection that the thimble gives is necessary for the finger which pushes the needle through, and also for the one underneath, which is likely to be pricked. You are probably familiar with conventional metal thimbles, but specialist quilting shops supply Japanese-style leather thimbles of various types.

Beeswax, available in blocks or small holders, is useful for strengthening your thread and prevents it twisting. You may also need an unpicking tool to rectify uneven stitching, particularly for machine quilting or embroidery.

Design Equipment

Designing Log Cabin patchwork is a very simple matter once you have learnt the basic technique. By altering or combining

Fabrics and threads for Log Cabin patchwork

different blocks, or by assembling them in a variety of ways, you will gradually feel confident to try out your own ideas.

Basic Drawing Equipment

For sketching and drafting ideas you will need a few basic drawing tools and materials such as a sketch pad or paper and a selection of pencils, crayons or felt-tips. Arithmetic, graph or dressmaker's squared drafting paper are used for working out

standard square blocks, and isometric paper is essential for designs based on hexagons, six-point diamonds and isosceles triangles.

Besides your quilter's rule, you will also need a standard 30cm (12in) ruler.

Fabrics and Threads

Fabric is the very essence of patchwork and in theory you can use almost any type for Log Cabin techniques. Successful projects can be made in cotton, silk, wool or synthetic fibres. In fact one of the great advantages of the technique, as opposed to some other patchwork methods, is that different weights and types can be used in a single project, provided you do not intend to launder it.

In years gone by recycled fabrics were used for quilts and covers, and you can still carry on this tradition by making 'memory' quilts from favourite clothes. If you decide to do this, choose the least worn areas of the garments and test their strength by pulling the fabrics in all directions. Using scrap fabrics left over from dressmaking or soft furnishing projects is also an option for creating an interesting and economical article, or you may be able to obtain sample books of fabrics from stores selling curtain materials.

Fabrics of natural fibres are usually easier to handle and less springy than synthetics, which sometimes are difficult to crease or press sharply. Manufacturers now produce cotton fabrics designed specially for patchwork projects. Specialist shops supply fabric packs of small amounts of fabric including coordinating and themed collections, together with different colourways of the same patterns. These are particularly useful for Log Cabin designs where the tonal values in the design are of the utmost importance.

There are also plain colours of every shade and hue. These are often available by mail order and most shops will send sample cards with swatches of their ranges for a small fee which can be set against your first purchase.

If the finished article is to be laundered, it is best to wash, dry and iron the fabrics before use, particularly some cottons which may shrink during the first washing. Dark fabrics should also be pre-washed to test the fastness of the dyes. It is not sensible to mix unwashed and pre-washed fabrics in the same project, as uneven shrinkage may occur.

Besides the conventional patchwork fabrics, you can also successfully use a wide range of different materials for Log Cabin. Thick tweeds work well with corduroys or woollens, lightweight silks, nylons and organzas can be combined with laces and ribbons.

Store the fabrics in their colour ranges so that they are easily accessible. Plastic boxes in the appropriate colour are a cheap and convenient option, or small pieces can be kept in large plastic confectionery jars or labelled shoe boxes.

Foundation Fabrics
Foundation or backing fabrics and linings should be chosen in tandem with the patchwork top, usually in a similar weight and fibre content. Light- or medium-weight calico, and plain or printed cotton poplin, sheeting or drill are all suitable. Wall-hangings require a heavier support, such as curtain lining, and they may also need to be interlined with non-woven interlining or canvas, particularly if they are not quilted.

Foundation/backing fabrics: curtain lining, cotton and calico

Synthetic wadding and needle-punch wadding

Wadding

If you decide to quilt your Log Cabin project, you will need a wadding which suits the work. Besides the fibre content of the wadding, the loft (thickness) is an important consideration, both for the look of the finished item and its intended use. The scale of the article should be considered and the appropriate loft evaluated. It should also be remembered that the more dense the quilting, the flatter the wadding will become.

Synthetic polyester wadding is available in several thicknesses with 50g (2oz) and 100g (4oz) being the most useful. It is practical for the majority of items as it is light weight, washable and may be dry-cleaned. It comes in several widths up to that suitable for a king-size bed quilt. Needle-punch polyester wadding is dense and firm with little loft, so it is a good choice for machine quilting and small-scale projects.

Fusible or iron-on fleece, which is good for lightly padded items, eliminates the need for tacking, but its main disadvantage is that the excess bulk in the seams is more tricky to cut away, as it has been fused to the seam allowance.

Silk, wool and cotton wadding, the

choice of those who wish to keep the fibre content of their projects uniform throughout, is available from specialist shops and handles well. However, these natural fibre waddings need careful laundering and produce a fairly flat effect.

Today, nearly all wadding is fire-retardant and has a slightly stiff feel; this can be eliminated, if necessary, by rinsing and drying. Although most wadding is white, specialist shops stock a grey one which is a good choice if you are working with dark fabrics.

Threads

There is a wide variety of threads on the market, all available in a large range of colours. Ordinary sewing threads come in cotton, silk and polyester and in various thicknesses; these are suitable for seaming Log Cabin either by hand or machine. It is usual, though not essential, to match the thread fibre to that of the fabric. Most patchworkers use cotton thread with cotton fabric, silk with silk, and polyester with polyester. However if your patchwork is constructed in mixed materials, you can choose the thread to coincide with the dominant fibre. The colour of the thread should tone or match the main colours of the design. For machine patchwork you can use a beige or grey thread throughout.

If you are quilting your design, specialist quilting thread, similar to buttonhole thread, gives more impact and greater durability than ordinary sewing thread. To decorate your work further, you can also use crochet cottons and embroidery threads such as stranded cotton, pearl cotton and coton à broder for additional effect.

BASIC INSTRUCTIONS

For successful piecing of Log Cabin patchwork you will need to master the basic techniques of cutting and stitching to produce an immaculate finish. As the method is made up of numerous strips of fabric seamed together, the cutting and stitching must be done with precision, because any inaccuracies will produce an uneven result and the finished Log Cabin blocks will not fit together.

Strips for all types of Log Cabin should be cut with the strips running either across or vertically down the straight grain. For bias bindings you will need to fold and cut on the bias, or use the diagonal line on the cutting mat as a guide.

Cutting Out

Using a Rotary Cutter

Rotary cutters are ideal for cutting strips and for simple geometric shapes such as the central squares or triangles. You can cut through one layer, or, with practice, through several layers. Before embarking on a project, always practise on a spare piece of fabric and make sure that the blade in your cutter is razor-sharp.

1 Square up the fabric before commencing, by laying it out smoothly on your cutting mat with the straight grain running vertically, and with the grid markings visible at the top and bottom. If you wish to cut through several layers, fold, refold and press the fabric carefully on the straight grain.

2 Align the quilter's rule vertically about 12mm (½in) from the right-hand raw edge of the fabric, using the grid markings, and hold it firmly. Release the safety guard on the cutter and, keeping the blade upright, start rolling the cutter away from you alongside the rule in one long movement across the mat. You may need to 'walk' your hand along the rule as you proceed. Remember to engage the safety gauge when you have completed the cut. Discard the cut strip.

3 If necessary realign the cut edge with a line on the cutting mat and, using the grid markings, place the rule at the desired width and use the cutter as above.

NB *If you prefer to use the marks on the quilter's rule to determine the width of the strip, work from left to right with the raw edge on the left. Reverse all these instructions if you are left-handed.*

Marking Fabric and Cutting with Scissors
If you do not possess a rotary cutter and mat, you can mark the fabric and cut it

out with scissors, though this is a slower method and should only be used for small projects.

A 6mm (¼in) seam allowance is needed for Log Cabin. If you are confident, this can be judged by eye, or you can mark it on the fabric using a quarter seamer. If you are machine piecing, the seam allowance can be gauged by using the width of the presser foot or altering the needle position accordingly.

Marking the fabric and cutting out

1 Lay the fabric out smoothly on a flat work surface, with the straight grain running vertically. Using a pencil or fabric marker and a ruler, measure and mark the width of the strip, including the seam allowances, in several places.

2 Place the ruler alongside the marks and draw a line.

3 Continue drawing more lines to the correct width and then cut out with sharp scissors.

NB *If you are using a quarter seamer as a guide for the seam allowance, it is best to mark this along both edges of the strips before cutting them out.*

Stitching

Hand Stitching

Running stitch is the main stitch used for seaming Log Cabin and is the alternative to machine stitching. The individual stitches should be small with equal spaces between them. You can also use running stitch for quilting.

For a satisfactory result, you will need to stitch neatly and accurately, making small evenly spaced stitches with a consistent seam allowance (see previous page).

Always check the accuracy of your seam allowance before attaching another strip. Failure to do this will only increase the problem and will result in a lopsided block.

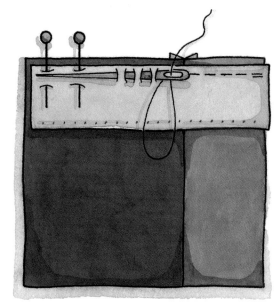

Running stitch

Running Stitch

1 Pin the strips in place, right sides together, with pins at right angles to the raw edge.

2 Use a thread which tones or matches the darker of the two fabrics. If in doubt, use a neutral colour such as beige or grey which blends well. Choose a needle appropriate to the fabric and thread.

3 Start with a double backstitch and, working from right to left if you are right-handed, bring the needle in and out of the layers of fabric. You can pick up two or three stitches before pulling the needle through. Finish with a double backstitch.

Machine Stitching

Although many people gain great satisfaction from working by hand, the speed of using a sewing machine for Log Cabin cannot be overlooked. With a little practice you should be able to achieve sufficient accuracy to give an immaculate finish without any loss of the traditional charm of hand work.

It is essential that you are totally familiar with your sewing machine and you should refer to your handbook to make sure that you understand how to check the tension so that you can produce smooth even stitches. It is a good idea to practise on a spare piece of fabric of similar weight and type to the project you are working on.

1 Pin the strips in place as for hand stitching (see facing page), with the pins at right angles to the raw edge.

2 Set the stitch width to 0 and the stitch length for normal stitching of approximately 10–12 stitches per 2.5cm (1in). As with hand stitching it is essential to keep a consistent seam allowance. You can stitch along a marked line, or use the width of the presser foot as a guide. Alter the needle position as necessary so that the needle pierces the fabric at the correct distance from the raw edge of the fabric, and the edge of the presser foot aligns exactly with the raw edge.

NB If you are unable to adjust the needle position, place a length of masking tape across the needle plate of the machine at the appropriate point, and align the raw edge with this. Some machines have markings engraved on the plate, which help to maintain a consistent seam allowance.

There is no need to double-stitch the beginning and end of each row of stitching as this will be held securely by the stitches of succeeding strips.

String (or Chain) Piecing

This is a quick method for piecing a group of identical Log Cabin blocks in 'assembly line' fashion (see page 36). Apart from the speed of execution, it is a way of keeping the blocks the same size, with consistent seam allowances. It can be used for multiple blocks of most shapes.

Pressing

For a professional finish it is essential to press the seams of the project as you proceed. For Log Cabin it is usual to press the seams to one side, away from the central square. Many patchworkers use their fingers to press hand stitching by pushing and smoothing the seam allowance to one side. This method may work well with crisp cotton fabrics, but ironing will produce a flatter more precise result.

If you are making a large machine-made project, set up your iron and ironing board close to the sewing machine so that you can press each seam as the work progresses.

DESIGN

Designing your own work is one of the joys of Log Cabin patchwork and, with very little experience and a basic knowledge of the technique, you will be able to create your own designs and projects. It is a good idea to become conversant with the particular method or Log Cabin variation but, when this expertise is achieved, there should be no barriers. You will find that, by arranging and rearranging the elements or blocks, you can create a successful and original design.

Selecting appropriate colours, patterns and texture adds to the excitement of the design, and there is a wealth of traditional patterns to study which can be developed and tried out with different colourways and emphasis. For a more formal approach, you can draft your designs on paper, so that you have an overall plan from which to work.

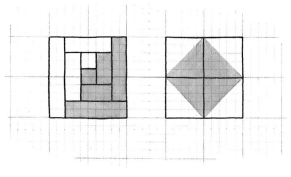

Drafting designs on square paper

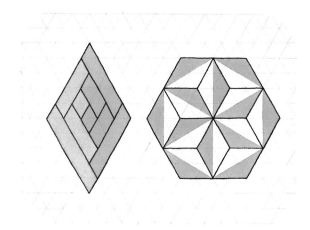

Drafting designs on isometric paper

DRAFTING DESIGNS ON PAPER AND COMPUTER

Designs on Paper

Log Cabin designs based on square or rectangular blocks can be drafted on squared arithmetic, graph or dressmaker's drafting paper. Isometric paper, made up of a series of isosceles triangles, is used for hexagonal, triangular and six-point diamond blocks.

A computer-generated print used for the centre square of a four-block design

On all these papers, the design is drawn and coloured in miniature using the squares or triangles as a guide for the finished project. Unless it is a very complicated design, there is no need to scale it up to its full size, though you should work out the size of both the central piece and the finished widths of the strips. Do not forget to add the appropriate seam allowances before cutting out the fabric.

A small project such as a bag or cushion can be designed using a single or double block. For larger projects there is a wide variety of different options.

The simplest of these is a repeat block with each one placed exactly as its neighbour. Alternating blocks are usually positioned with every other one reversed or mirrored. To judge a mirrored effect, place a single block alongside a looking-glass or

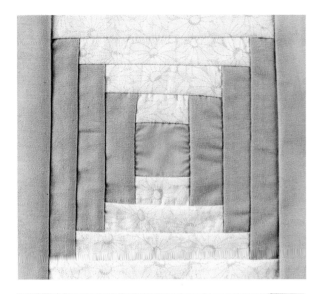

Two blocks using the same fabrics but in different arrangements. Above, a traditional Courthouse Steps block, and below, a variation of Round the Houses

Computer Design

There are several specialist computer programs available which deal with patchwork design in general. These offer a quick and simple method of drafting designs, particularly for large-scale repeated block projects, as you can easily alter the colours and size to your liking and rotate and mirror the blocks at will. Some programs have an in-built library of traditional patterns and borders which can be adapted or used as given. They will even print out templates with added seam allowances and estimate the yardage for each fabric. These make a good starting point for designs and are an easy way of assessing relative tonal values and colour emphasis.

hand mirror so that the design is reflected in reverse. Diagonally constructed blocks can be placed in any of four positions with the dark part at any corner. A further option is to place the blocks 'on point', that is in diamond formation.

Some Log Cabin designs are also suitable for use as borders for quilts, wallhangings, garments or accessories.

COLOUR

Choosing the colour for a project is a very personal affair. Most people have their favourite colours and combination of shades, and this will influence their choice of fabric. Indeed, colour may well act as your main starting point. For example, you may wish to make a quilt to coordinate with the other soft furnishings in your bedroom, or to create table mats to match your kitchen or dining-room chinaware. You can learn from the way professional textile and product designers use colour in varying proportions and you may discover unexpected combinations of different

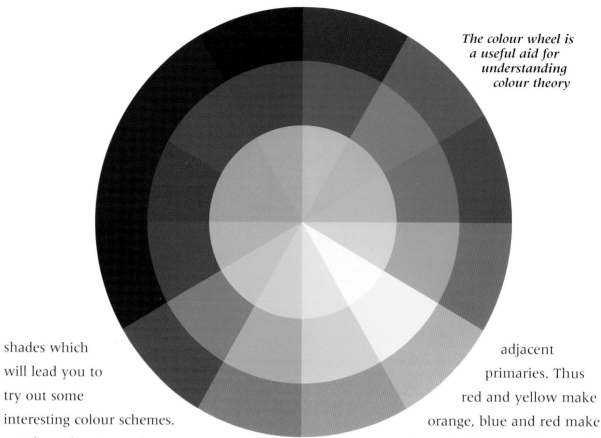

shades which will lead you to try out some interesting colour schemes.

When planning a design, experiment with different colourways and try out the colours in different positions in a block. The emphasis will be changed and sometimes unexpected and interesting results will emerge.

Basic Colour Principles

If you have an understanding of the basic principles of colour and tone, you are more likely to be able to develop your own colour ideas and to produce tonally balanced projects. The colour wheel is a device showing the colours of the rainbow arranged in a circle. Placed equidistant on the wheel are the primary colours – the pure hues of red, yellow and blue. Between these are the secondary colours which combine equal quantities of the two adjacent primaries. Thus red and yellow make orange, blue and red make purple, and yellow and blue make green. You will notice that on one side of the circle are the warm reds and yellows and on the other are the cool greens and blues. On the inside of the wheel are tints, that is paler versions, while on the outer perimeter are shades, which are darker. Thus pink is a tint and burgundy is a shade of red.

Colours which are close together on the colour wheel, such as blue and green, together with their respective tints and shades, are known as harmonious. These blend well together and create an undemanding and restful design. Those which are on opposite sides of the wheel, such as red and green, purple and yellow, and blue and orange are known as complementary colours. These, together with black and white, give strong contrasts, so designs using these will be more vibrant and eye-catching than those with harmonious colours. A combination of harmonious and contrasting colours in different proportions can give a particularly pleasing result. Indeed a small amount of contrast can enliven an otherwise uninteresting piece of work.

Tonal Value

The importance of tonal value in Log Cabin patchwork cannot be over-emphasized. Traditional designs such as Barn Raising and Straight Furrow rely for their visual impact on differently toned fabrics placed diagonally on opposite sides of the block.

For designs based on Courthouse Steps the emphasis is vertical or horizontal.

Tonality is the intensity of colour – whether it is light or dark – and is defined by studying the tints and shades on the colour wheel. For example cream is a lighter tone than yellow and navy blue a darker tone than pale pink. To assess the relative tonal values of a selection of fabrics, place them alongside one another and look at them at a distance through half-closed eyes. The lighter tones will reflect the light and stand out more than the darker tones which absorb it and will therefore recede. It can be more difficult to gauge the tonal value of patterned fabrics, but with practice you will be able to assess the effect.

Using the back of a printed fabric reduces the intensity of colour

You can sometimes use the back of a fabric to reduce the intensity of its colour, or for some projects you may be able to overlay the fabric with a transparent organza or net. Shiny fabrics such as satin, which reflect the light, will show up more than dark, dull fabrics such as wool, which absorb it.

Shot fabrics – usually of silk or shiny synthetic fibres – present interesting possibilities, as they are woven with the warp in one colour and the weft in another. If two strips are stitched at right-angles to one another, the light falling on them will show up the different colours and produce an iridescent three-dimensional effect. Fabrics made from metallic fibres are particularly lively and dynamic. On some woven fabrics, such as brocade, the design is completely reversed on the back, so that those areas that are shiny on one side appear dull on the other, and vice versa. This characteristic can be explored with interesting results.

Dyeing Fabrics

Although there are many different coloured fabrics available today, it is sometimes exciting to dye your own, and manufacturers have made life easy with ranges of dyes for all sorts of fabrics. Simply follow the instructions carefully, checking the fabric content to ensure that the correct type of dye is used.

Make a note of the fabric's weight and the amount of dye used, so that you can repeat the effect if necessary. In general, hot-water dyes are suitable for natural fibres (including wool and silk), viscose rayon and nylon, while cold-water dyes are best for cotton, linen and rayon, with lighter shades on wool, silk and polycotton.

With a little practice, and by over-dyeing, you can create a large selection of colours, and by leaving the pieces of fabric in the dye-bath for ever-increasing periods of time you can achieve a wide range of tones. You can also dye a group of different printed fabrics the same colour, then use them together or in separate projects with a harmonious effect.

The more advanced dyeing techniques such as batik and tie-dye are also a possibility, as the patterns created can be isolated for central Log Cabin squares or strips cut from the dyed fabrics.

SAFETY RULES FOR DYEING

- Work in a well-ventilated room.
- Read the manufacturer's instructions very carefully.
- Wear rubber gloves and a mask or respirator if you are working on a large project, as dyes can be harmful if inhaled.
- Cover your work surface and surrounding areas with plastic and newspaper.
- Clean up any spills immediately with kitchen paper.

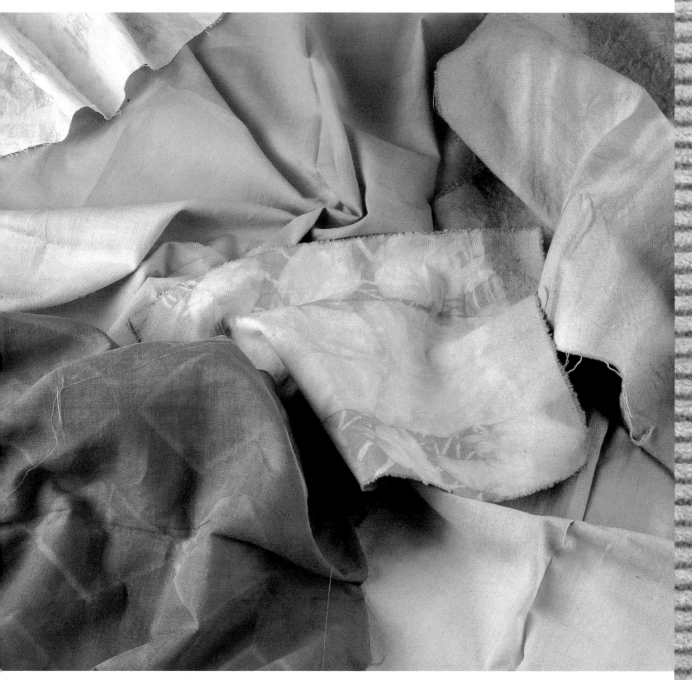

A selection of tie-dyed, batik and dyed fabrics

Another method of dyeing is to use natural dyes. Some of the plant materials such as onion skins, tea and coffee, are readily available all year round, whilst others such as golden rod and blackberry are seasonal. These give a soft luminous effect and are ideal for over-dyeing light-coloured fabrics or for taking the brightness from an over-dominant colour. Many natural dyes require a mordant such as alum, tin or chrome to assist in making the dyes fast. Mordants also produce different shades of colour.

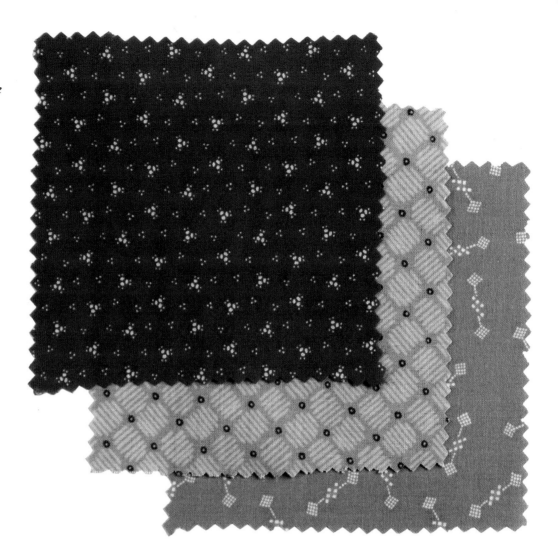

Small-scale prints

PATTERN

Although some people prefer to use plain colours exclusively, there are many exciting printed fabrics. These range from those produced specially for patchwork, to dress and furnishing materials. They can be used together or in combination with plains. You should select patterned fabrics, not only for their colour, but also for the tone, density and scale. You should therefore view them both at close range and from a distance, in order to determine the relative tonal values. The scale of the pattern should also be assessed in relation to the width and length of the Log Cabin strips and to the design as

a whole. All-over designs with small closely packed flowers or motifs may appear as a muted blur from a distance, with the actual pattern indistinguishable, whereas fabrics which contain a lot of contrast, including white, will be more dominant. These can be more difficult to use, as they draw the eye to them in a way which may not be intended.

Pattern Categories

Patterned fabrics can be divided into several categories. Some prints have very muted shaded and dyed effects with very little contrast, and these can replace a plain fabric. Small prints with tiny floral or spot-motif patterns are often over-used and, although they are useful, an entire project of this type of fabric can be rather bland and uninteresting.

Medium prints are usually busier than small prints and may have an all-over pattern giving good depth of tone. Fabrics, such as large-scale florals or chintzes, can be more challenging and those with strongly contrasting colours should be used with care. However, it may be possible, with careful cutting, to select those parts of the pattern to suit your requirements.

Directional prints, such as stripes and border prints, can be very dominant, but give plenty of scope for creativity with the stripes running either vertically across, or lengthwise along, the strips. Unless you are very experienced it is not a good idea to attempt using the stripes running diagonally, if they are not printed in this way, as bias cutting will cause the strips to stretch.

Interesting optical effects can be achieved using striped fabrics, but it is essential to cut and stitch with great precision so that the stripes match up.

Medium-scale prints

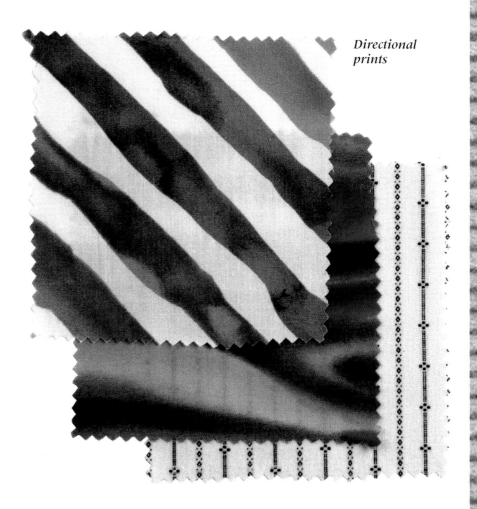

Directional prints

Creating Your Own Patterned Fabric

There are a large number of ways of producing your own individual patterns on fabric, including painting, drawing, stamping, stencilling and printing. These methods usually work best on smooth-surfaced fabrics, but you may like to experiment on those with more texture.

Although in theory you can draw or paint with a number of ordinary paints, felt-tips and crayons, in most cases a more satisfactory result can be achieved by using specialist products which do not stiffen the fabric, will retain their fastness

The central square of this block is stencilled and the Log Cabin border is tie-dyed

and can be washed or dry-cleaned. It is always advisable to wash new fabric before use, as it usually contains a dressing that may adversely affect the stability of the paint.

Fabric Paints and Crayons
Fabric paints offer limitless opportunities for experimentation as they can be spattered, sprayed, sponged or used with rubber stamps. There are a number of different makes and types but the most useful are all-purpose fabric paints. These are available in a range of basic colours, plus iridescent, pearlized and metallic finishes. The colours are intermixable so you can start with a small selection of primary colours, plus black and white. They are suitable for the majority of fabrics and most types are made fast by pressing with a hot iron. You can apply them with a brush or sponge, or try spattering, spraying or stencilling.

For a more detailed, spontaneous or delicate approach, fabric markers are a good addition or alternative to paints. There are several types including pens, crayons, oil-paint sticks and paint tubes. Fabric pens are used in exactly the same way as felt-tip pens and come in a wide range of colours and widths so are suitable for fine or heavy lines. Crayons are similar to wax crayons and are available in a small range of colours which can be overlaid or blended with the fingers to produce other hues. They are best used on natural fibres or those with little synthetic content, as they need to withstand ironing at a high temperature in order to set the colour. Oil-paint sticks are chunky card-covered crayons made from a mixture of wax and oil paint and come in a wide range of colours, including metallics. They can be blended to create a huge range of different effects and become permanent after about 48 hours when they should be ironed to fix the colour. Glitter and puff paint tubes produce three-dimensional raised effects in glossy, pearlized and sparkling finishes in a limited range of interesting colours. They are applied directly from the tube and can be washed by hand after 72 hours. The puff paints should be allowed to dry and then pressed with a hot iron on the reverse side to make them expand.

Transfer Printing
There are several different ways of transferring patterns and images onto fabric and the results can be useful for both central motifs or for strips. One of the main advantages of transfer printing is that you can use ready-made designs. However, you should remember that some pictures may be subject to copyright and may not be used without prior permission. In most cases the images will appear on the fabric in reverse, so you should take this fact into consideration when selecting a picture. In each case follow the manufacturer's instructions carefully. Transfer printing methods with transfer paints and crayons, laser transfers, or photocopied transfers are

all possible, though some products are only suitable for use on fabrics which contain a large proportion of synthetic fibres, whilst others work best on natural fabrics.

Computer transfers of clip-art, scanned photos, or your own computer-generated designs can be made by using a special transfer paper suitable for ink-jet printers.

Commercially produced rubber stamps decorate the fabric and the central appliqué motif for this Chimneys and Corners design

Block Printing and Stamping

This ancient method of transferring decorative motifs and patterns to fabric is associated mainly with India and the Far East, where wooden blocks are carved with intricate designs. You may be able to purchase a selection of these but they tend to be rare and therefore expensive. However, blocks and stamps can be made from a variety of different materials, such as potatoes and other vegetables, leaves and flowers, string or card stuck to a block, or plastic sponge cut into shape.

The craft of rubber stamping has seen a growth in popularity in recent years for all types of paper crafts and you can purchase stamps in a wide range of designs. Some of these are suitable for fabric printing, but you should experiment first with the fabric paint and stamp in order to get a clear image. Generally it is best to choose bold designs, rather than intricate subjects with delicate imagery. Alternatively, you can make your own simple stamps using rubber or plastic erasers cut to shape with a craft knife.

Marbling

Marbling is a technique which bookbinders have used for centuries for decorative covers and endpapers. To create marbled

Marbled fabrics are combined with plain cottons

fabrics in the traditional way is extremely skilful, but you can now purchase marbling kits which offer a simple way of reproducing the characteristic swirling and feathered designs.

These products have a limited range of colours, but can be intermixed to extend the effects. They work well on most fabrics and are made fast by ironing. Apart from the paints and gel, you will need a flat plastic dish such as a cat litter or photographic tray, some cocktail sticks and a home-made comb made from a lath of wood, with nails tacked along one edge.

Follow the manufacturer's instructions for preparing the gel and leave for one hour. Place drops of marbling paint onto the surface of the gel and move the colours about with the comb or sticks to create the desired pattern. Lay the fabric on the surface, remove, rinse and allow to dry before ironing to set the colour.

TEXTURE

Although Log Cabin patchwork is usually associated with the arrangement of pattern and colour, the texture of the fabrics can give an additional emphasis or interest in a

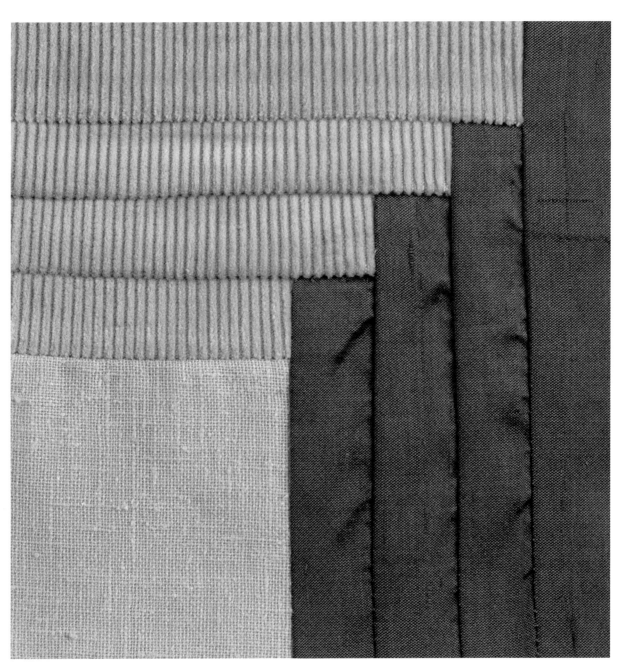

Textured fabrics can add an extra dimension to a project – corduroy, tweed, or glazed cotton are all possibilities

project. You may choose to make a complete article in one colour but using a range of different textures.

The actual construction of some fabrics is inherently textural – they may be woven with a slub, bouclé, or hairy surface; they may be closely or loosely woven, and others, such as velvet, corduroy or towelling, possess a pile. Some finishing processes, such as glazing, produce an alternative surface texture, such as sheen or sparkle. Satin and some silk and rayon fabrics possess a characteristic shine.

Textures can be emphasized by contrast, that is by placing a smooth, shiny area close to a dull, rough fabric – velvet next to silk, tweed adjacent to cotton. The effects of light and shade in a work can be accentuated by the imaginative use of different textures. Smooth shiny fabrics will reflect the light, while dull fabrics absorb it and are more likely to recede. These characteristics can be fully exploited in Log Cabin designs, particularly for projects such as wallhangings, where the practicalities of washing and ironing do not need to be taken into consideration.

An alternative way of adding texture to a Log Cabin project is to use lace, braid or frayed edges instead of the traditional fabric strips (see page 69). You can also include inserted embellishments such as prairie points (see page 73), piping, or frills (see pages 91–2).

TRADITIONAL
TECHNIQUES

BASIC CONSTRUCTION

The basic technique of Log Cabin patchwork involves stitching strips of fabric around a central square to form a larger square known as a block. This block can be used alone, or joined with others to form different patterns for a larger piece of work.

Log Cabin can be stitched by hand or by machine, and the blocks can be sewn individually or string-pieced by machine for greater accuracy and speed, a method which is particularly useful if you are making a large-scale project such as a quilt or wallhanging.

As with all patchwork, it is essential to work with precision and accuracy so that the strips and blocks fit together. Follow the cutting instructions using a rotary cutter or scissors (see page 12), taking great care to cut out the fabrics to exact widths and to stitch with a consistent seam allowance (see page 13). The strips can be cut in long lengths and then

trimmed to fit the block as you proceed. Although a certain amount of fabric may be wasted, this is compensated for as there is no need to work out the exact lengths beforehand. The task is therefore much quicker and more accurate. Always check that the block is not lopsided as you proceed with each strip, as failure to do this will only increase the inaccuracy.

Many conventional forms of Log Cabin rely for their effect upon the use of contrasting toned fabrics. These are usually placed diagonally opposite one another within the blocks, so that when arranged in different formations they produce a wide variety of designs. These include the traditional patterns of Starry Night, Barn Raising, Straight Furrow and Streak of Lightning (see pages 37–8).

One of the advantages of Log Cabin is that you can use different types of fabric in a single project although, if it is likely to be laundered, it is best to keep to fabric of similar fibre content.

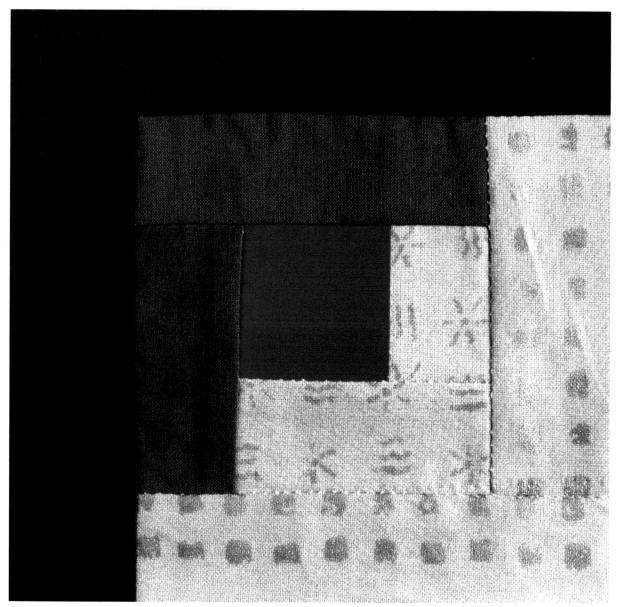

A basic construction block with light and dark fabrics placed diagonally for strong emphasis

Making a Basic Block

1 Cut two sets of long 4cm (1½in) wide strips in contrasting tones and a 4cm (1½in) central square.

2 With right sides together, pin and stitch a light-coloured strip along one side of the square. If stitching by hand, use tiny running stitches (see page 14). For machine stitching, work straight stitches using the edge of the machine foot as a gauge to maintain the 6mm (¼in) seam allowance. Trim off the excess and press the seam away from the centre.

3 Working in a clockwise direction, stitch the second light-coloured strip across the trimmed end of the first strip and along

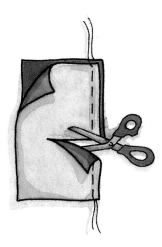

Stitching the first strip to the centre square

the second side of the square. Trim and press as before.

4 Continue with the third and fourth sides in the darker-coloured strips to complete the square. At each stage check that the seam allowance is accurate and that the block is square.

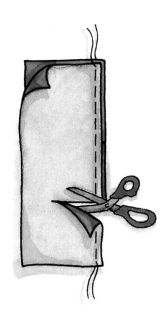

Stitching the second strip

5 Always working in a clockwise direction, continue stitching two light and two dark strips on diagonally opposite sides of the block until you have achieved the required size.

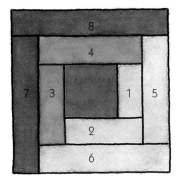

Assembling the strips in a clockwise direction

6 Work several blocks in the same way, so that they are ready to be joined in the desired arrangement.

Joining the Blocks

There are a number of ways of making a simple arrangement of four blocks suitable for a cushion or a small bag. You can either draft the design (see page 17) or rearrange the finished blocks to your satisfaction. If you prefer the latter, you will need to make up a number of finished blocks and then pin them to a board or larger piece of fabric to assess the result. Larger projects can be attempted in a similar fashion.

1 To complete an arrangement of four blocks, stitch two blocks with right sides together, matching the seams as

necessary, and maintaining the 6mm (¼in) seam allowance.

2 Repeat with two more blocks and join these to the first two to form a square.

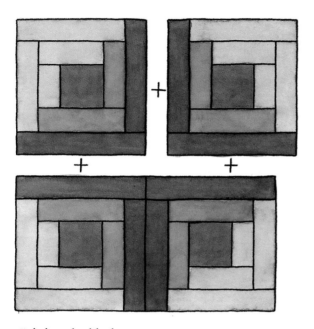

Joining the blocks

3 For larger projects, such as quilts or wallhangings, join a series of blocks with vertical seams to form horizontal larger lengths, and then stitch these lengths together to form a large rectangle.

4 At each stage check the accuracy of the seam allowances.

String Piecing

If you are making a large-scale project by machine, such as a quilt which involves a number of identical blocks, the quickest and most efficient way to do this is by string (or chain) piecing.

1 With right sides together, place a series of centre squares on a light-coloured strip, leaving a small gap between each square. Stitch the two fabrics together along one side of the squares. Press the seam away from the centre and cut the pieces apart, trimming away any excess as necessary.

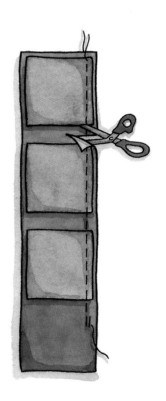

String piecing the centre squares to the first strip

2 With right sides together, place the stitched pieces along a second light-coloured strip with the square at the bottom and stitch as before. Press and cut apart to size.

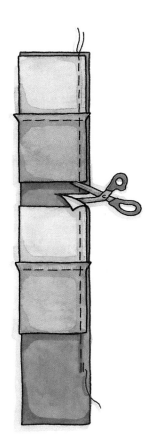

Stitching the second strip

3 Continue by turning the stitched pieces anti-clockwise each time, adding the third and fourth dark strips. This will complete the first round.

4 Proceed by adding two light and two dark strips on opposite sides of the block until the required size is achieved. The blocks are now ready to be stitched together (see above).

TRADITIONAL DESIGNS OF BASIC CONSTRUCTION

For these traditional designs the blocks, with their strongly defined diagonal contrasts, are arranged so that the dark area of each one is aligned with the dark area of an adjacent block to form a diagonal shape, or dark stripe.

Starry Night is the simplest design consisting of four repeated blocks with the darker areas placed together to form a diamond shape. The set of four blocks can be used alone for a cushion, or repeated for a quilt or throw (see below).

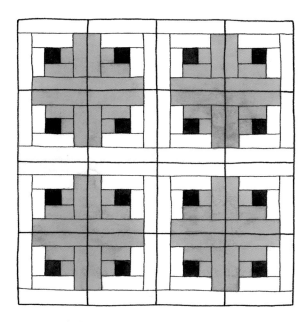

Starry Night

The Straight Furrow design (overleaf) is suitable for larger projects of at least four rows of four blocks. On the first row, the first block has the dark side at bottom right and the second block has the dark side at the top left. Repeat this arrangement across the width of the quilt. For the second row, the first block has the dark on the top left and the second block has the dark at the bottom right. Repeat these two rows and stitch them together to create the diagonal stripe.

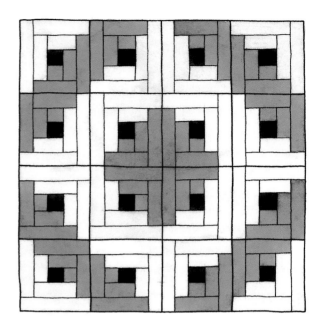

Barn Raising

Streak of Lightning (below) with its strong zigzag pattern is the most complex of these four traditional designs. For the first row each pair of blocks has the dark area of the first block at top right, placed next to the dark area of the second block at bottom left. For the second row these mirror the first,

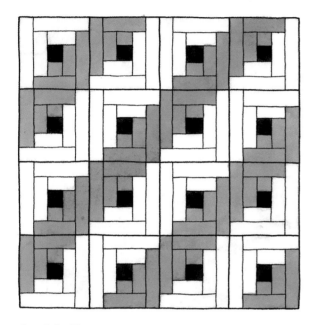

Straight Furrow

The Barn Raising design (top right) is a favourite for large-scale quilts or wallhangings of at least eight rows of eight blocks. Proceed as for the Straight Furrow design which is used for the top left-hand quarter of the project. For the top right-hand quarter the blocks are arranged so that they mirror the adjacent quarter. The bottom two quarters then mirror the top two, so that the diagonal emphasis results in a diamond pattern of dark stripes.

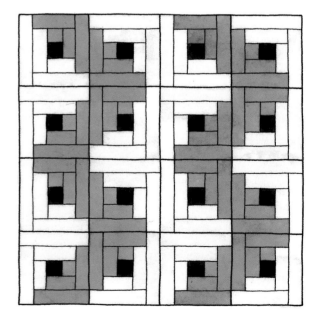

Streak of Lightning

so that the first pair of blocks has the dark area of the first block at bottom right, placed next to the dark area of the second block at top left. These two rows are then repeated down the length of the quilt. For an effective result there should be at least four rows of four blocks. The Streak of Lightning design can be adapted to form larger zigzags across the width of the quilt.

Chimneys and Corners

This design (also called Chimney Corners), is developed from the basic Log Cabin square block. The emphasis is on the diagonal pattern of small squares included at one end of every alternate strip. Careful cutting and stitching is essential for the success of this method, as the small squares must match perfectly. The blocks can be used in pairs for a zigzag pattern to emerge, or assembled so that the design develops in a similar fashion to Straight Furrow or Barn Raising.

The variation Chimney Corners with Nine-patch Centre (see page 45) is constructed in the Courthouse Steps formation.

1 Cut a selection of light and dark 4cm (1½in) strips, two light and two dark 4cm (1½in) squares, plus a number of 4cm (1½in) squares in a contrasting fabric.

2 With right sides together, stitch a contrast square to a light square and another to a dark square, and then stitch these together in chequerboard fashion.

Adding the first two strips for Chimneys and Corners

3 With right sides together, stitch a light-coloured strip along the top edge of the block. Trim off the excess and press the seam away from the centre.

4 Stitch a contrast square to the end of the second (dark) strip, and, working in a clockwise direction, stitch the strip and the square to the right-hand side of the block, matching the seams carefully.

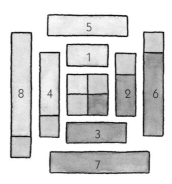

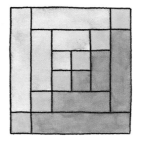

Assembling in a clockwise direction

5 Add a dark strip (without a square) to the bottom of the block.

The brightly coloured squares stand out against the duller fabrics to stress the diagonal pattern of Chimneys and Corners

6 Add a light strip with a square to the left-hand side of the block.

7 Continue in this way until the desired size is achieved.

Round the Houses

The simplicity of this design is achieved with a series of concentric stripes around the central square of the traditional Log

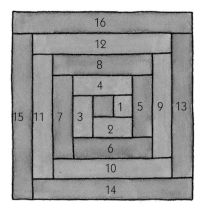

Assembling Round the Houses in a clockwise direction

Cabin block. The four strips in each row around the square are usually in identical fabric, or in one which is very close in tone and hue. These can contrast with the previous four, or harmonize to give a gradual change in tonal value.

COURTHOUSE STEPS BLOCKS

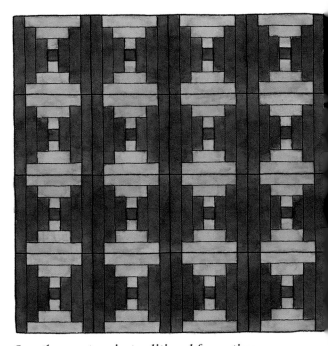

Courthouse steps in traditional formation

Traditional Courthouse Steps

Although this is a traditional Log Cabin design the construction differs from the basic block as, instead of assembling the strips in a spiral around the square, they are placed alternately top and bottom and then on right and left sides. When the blocks are joined together, it results in a vertical or horizontal pattern which is less bold than the diagonal formation, as the block is visually divided into four sections

The contrasting plain and patterned fabrics emphasize the effect of this Round the Houses block

instead of two. For a more spontaneous design, the blocks can be placed in random directions and the tonal values varied. You can also string-piece this method.

1 Cut two sets of 4cm (1½in) strips in contrasting tones, and a 4cm (1½in) central square. It is easier and more accurate to cut the strips in long lengths and trim them as required after stitching.

2 With right sides together, stitch a light-coloured strip along the top edge of the square. If stitching by hand use tiny running stitches (see page 14). For machine stitching, work straight stitches using the

edge of the machine foot as a gauge to maintain the 6mm (¼in) seam allowance. Trim off the excess and press the seam away from the centre.

3 Stitch the second light-coloured strip across the bottom edge of the square, trim and press as before.

4 Stitch the third and fourth dark-coloured strips along the two remaining opposite sides of the square and along the trimmed strips. At each stage be sure to check that the seam allowance is accurate, and that the block is square, then press the seam away from the centre.

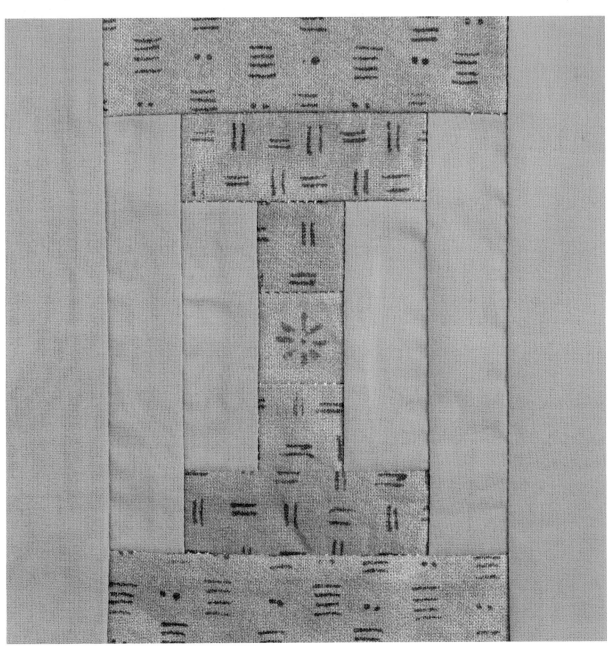

A combination of plain and patterned fabrics for the traditional Courthouse Steps method

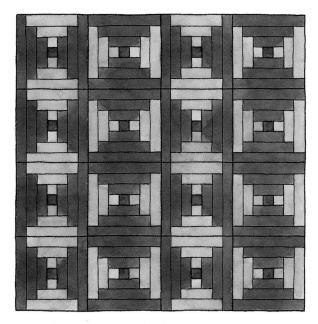

Courthouse Steps with alternating blocks

5 Continue stitching two light and two dark strips on opposite sides of the block until the required size is achieved.

6 Work several blocks in the same way, so that they are ready to be joined in the desired arrangement. The emphasis of the dark-toned fabrics can be vertical or horizontal, or the blocks can be pieced together randomly for a less rigid result.

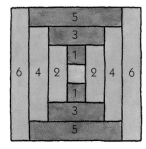

Piecing diagram, showing how to assemble Courthouse Steps

Greek Key Pattern

Although this is known as the Greek Key design, this spiral motif can be found in the ancient artefacts of Central and South America, China and Japan. It is also a familiar pattern in Celtic art. The method of construction is similar to Courthouse Steps, but the effect is very different. Just two contrasting fabrics are needed and the block can be stitched together as a border, or used for larger projects with the pattern repeated, mirrored, or rotated (see illustration overleaf).

1 Cut two sets of 4cm (1½in) strips in contrasting tones, and two 4cm (1½in) central squares in the same two contrasting tones. It is easier and more accurate to cut the strips in long lengths and trim them as required after stitching

2 Stitch the two contrasting squares together, with right sides facing. If stitching by hand use tiny running stitches. For machine stitching, work straight stitches using the edge of the machine foot as a gauge to maintain the 6mm (¼in) seam allowance. Trim off the excess and press the seam away from the centre

3 With the dark square at the top and the right sides together, stitch a dark-coloured strip across the right-hand side and a light-coloured strip across the left-hand, opposite, side. Trim and press as before.

The use of light and dark fabrics shows up the spiralling Greek Key pattern

4 Stitch a second light-coloured strip across the top and a second dark-coloured strip across the bottom.

5 Continue stitching dark and light-coloured strips on opposite sides of the square so that the design spirals from the centre.

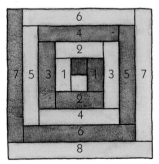

Piecing diagram, showing how to assemble the Greek Key pattern to form a square

Chimney Corners with Nine-patch Centre

This design evolves from Chimney and Corners (see page 39), resulting in a series of small squares criss-crossing the block. The centre is made up of nine squares in a chequerboard formation, and the subsequent strips with squares stitched at either side with plain strips at top and bottom. Careful attention must be paid to seam allowances and matching of the seams.

The understated printed pattern on the small squares does not detract from the overall effect of the Chimney Corners with Nine-patch Centre

1 Cut four 4cm (1½in) squares in light-coloured fabric, and 13 the same size in dark-coloured fabric. Cut some 4cm (1½in) strips in light-coloured fabric.

2 Assemble four light and five dark squares in chequer-board formation.

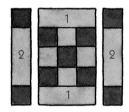

Assembling the Nine-patch Centre and the first row

3 Add light-coloured strips to the top and bottom edges.

4 Stitch a dark-coloured square to the beginning and end of the next strip, then stitch to the right-hand edge, matching seams.

5 Add a similar strip with squares to the left-hand edge.

6 Continue stitching light strips to the top and bottom of the block and strips, with dark squares at the beginning and end of each at either side of the block, until the required size is achieved.

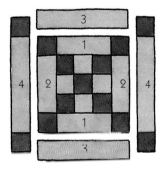

Assembling the block

VARIATIONS

CURVES AND CIRCULAR EFFECTS

Although traditional Log Cabin designs tend to be based on a 90° diagonal emphasis, you can create a series of curves, quarter- and semi-circles with a little adjustment to the original method. The standard quarter-circle block is made up of two sets of strips, with the more dominant fabric being cut twice as wide as that of paler tonal value. This block can be repeated and arranged in a variety of different ways.

Single quarter, or double semi-circular blocks can be used alone, or repeated across a large-scale project. Four quarter-circles placed together to form a circle make an ideal design for a square cushion, or for a repeat motif.

For a more random effect the width of the strips can be varied to produce a wealth of different designs.

Curves and circular effects can also be adjusted to incorporate two small rectangles, instead of the usual squares, at

Left **Rio Street Dance** *by Flavin Glover. Diamond Log Cabin, machine-pieced and hand quilted*

the centre of the quarter-circle block, so that a quarter-oval results. This elongated block can then be used to produce oval shapes for a quilt or throw. For experiments with circles use the traditional method of assembly, but for ovals it is best to use the Courthouse Steps method.

1 Cut a similar number of dark-toned 4cm (1½in) strips and light-toned 2cm (¾in) strips, plus a 4cm (1½in) square in both light- and dark-toned fabrics.

2 Stitch the two squares together, with right sides facing. Press the seam away from the centre.

3 Working in a clockwise direction, and keeping the light-toned square on the left, stitch a dark-toned, wide strip across the bottom edge of the two squares. Trim and press as before.

4 Using the narrow light-toned stripes, complete the left and top sides to form the square. At each stage check that the seam allowance is accurate and that the block is square.

A quarter-circle block clearly shows the curved effect of this technique

Sixteen quarter-oval repeated and reflected blocks

5 Always working in a clockwise direction, continue stitching two wide, dark strips and two narrow, light strips on diagonally opposite sides of the block, until the required size is achieved.

6 You will notice that a curve has emerged and the original square is now off-centre.

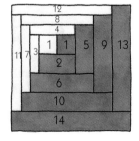

Piecing diagram for assembling a circular-effect block

RECTANGLES

This variation of the standard block starts with a rectangle, rather than a square, in the centre. The strips are stitched as for the basic method (see page 34–5) or the Courthouse Steps method (see page 40–3), so that the finished block is a rectangle. This can be used as a single unit for a small project such as a table mat, cushion or bag, or joined together in similar formations as the traditional blocks, resulting in a more elongated design.

This can be a useful way of resolving a design such as a wall-hanging which needs to be rectangular in shape. The traditional designs such as Barn Raising and Straight Furrow (see page 38) can be adapted easily, as can Courthouse Steps and its variations such as the Greek Key pattern (see page 43).

Rectangular blocks can be set either horizontally or vertically, or an alternative is to set them on point. This can be done in two ways. For the first, the rows of blocks can be stitched together in the normal way and then turned on point with the excess cut away to form straight vertical and

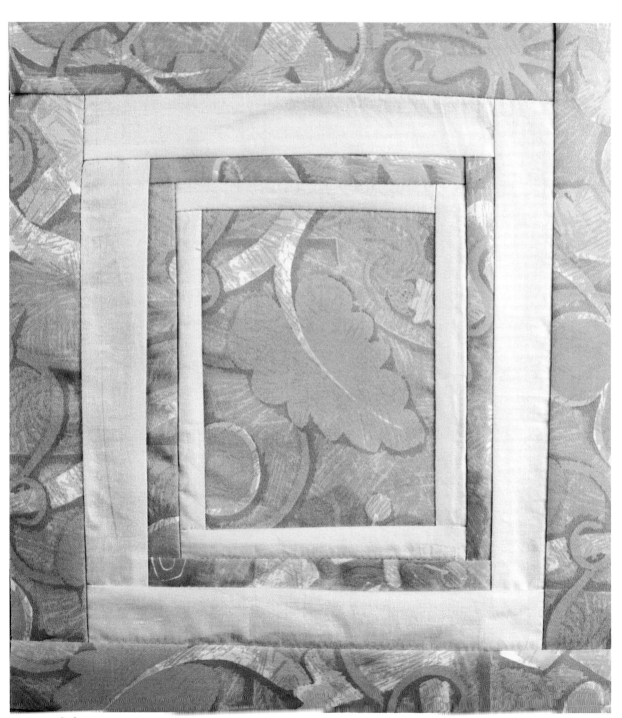

A Round the Houses block is varied with rectangular centre and strips of different widths

Assembling a rectangular block with narrow and wide strips in Courthouse Steps formation

horizontal edges. For the second method, the blocks are stitched together in vertical formation. The second and subsequent strip of blocks is stitched to the previous strip so that the design is in stepped formation. It is essential to measure the exact distance of this step and to repeat it for each subsequent row.

Elongated rectangles, placed on point in stepped formation

PINEAPPLE PATTERN BLOCKS

The designs based on the traditional Pineapple pattern continue the original technique of strips around a central square, but with the addition of contrasting strips forming trapeziums or triangles at each corner. As with all Log Cabin methods, careful stitching and measuring is essential to the success of the design. Single blocks can be effective, or they can be repeated in straight rows, or on point.

Basic Pineapple Pattern

1 Cut an 8cm (3in) square of light-coloured fabric, and two similar squares of a contrasting fabric diagonally, to produce four right-angled triangles. Cut a selection of 5cm (2in) wide strips in the two contrasting fabrics.

2 Mark the centre of each side of the square, and the centre of the long sides of the triangles. With right sides together,

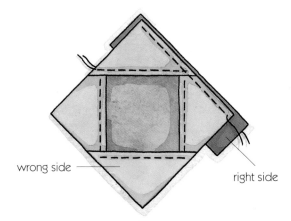

wrong side ——

right side

Stitching the first light-coloured strip to the square with the triangles

A basic Pineapple Pattern block using plain and patterned fabrics

stitch a triangle centrally along one side of the square and press away from the centre.

3 Stitch a second triangle on the opposite side of the centre square and then repeat on the remaining two sides to produce a larger square.

4 Place the square with the attached triangles face down on a light-coloured strip, and stitch together through the point of the triangle (see diagram on facing page).

5 Repeat with a light-coloured strip on the other three sides, then trim across

the ends of the strips at exactly 45°, with the cutting line parallel to the central square, to form an octagon (see below).

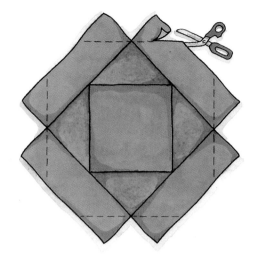

Trimming at 45° across the ends of each strip

6 Stitch four dark-coloured strips along each side. Trim at 45° as before.

7 Continue in this way, stitching alternately light- and dark-coloured rows of four strips around the block until the desired size is achieved.

Piecing diagram for Pineapple Pattern

8 Finish with a triangle or a series of strips at each corner to form a square.

Spiral Pineapple Pattern

This spiral design is a combination of the basic Pineapple pattern and the Greek Key pattern (see page 43). The arrangement of colours differs from the basic Pineapple pattern, because the strips in contrasting colours are placed opposite one another around the central square. The stitching method, however, is exactly the same.

1 Cut an 8cm (3in) square of coloured fabric and two similar squares of two contrasting fabrics diagonally, to produce two each of four right-angled triangles. Cut a selection of 5cm (2in) wide strips in the two contrasting fabrics.

2 Mark the centre of each side of the square and the centre of the long sides of the triangles. With right sides together, stitch a light-coloured triangle centrally along one side of the square, then press away from the centre.

3 Stitch a dark-coloured triangle on the opposite side of the centre square and then repeat on the remaining two sides, with light- and dark-coloured triangles opposite one another to produce a larger square.

4 Place the square, with the triangles attached, face down on a light-

Combining a plain and a patterned fabric produces a striking Spiral Pineapple effect

coloured strip, and stitch together through the point of the triangle.

5 Repeat with a dark-coloured strip on the opposite side. Trim across the ends of the strips at exactly 45° to form a square, keeping the cutting line parallel to the central square.

6 Add two more light- and dark-coloured strips opposite one another and trim as above.

7 Continue in this way until the desired size is achieved, stitching light- and dark-coloured strips on opposite sides of the square to form the spiral design.

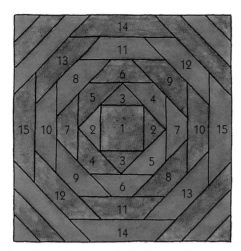

Piecing diagram for Spiral Pineapple

8 Trim to form a square, or add triangles cut to size at each corner.

Flying Geese Pattern

This differs from the basic Pineapple pattern as triangles of similar size are placed at each corner of the square and its subsequent strips. As with similar patterns, it can be used as a single unit or repeated for large-scale projects.

A harmonious choice of colour is used for this Flying Geese design

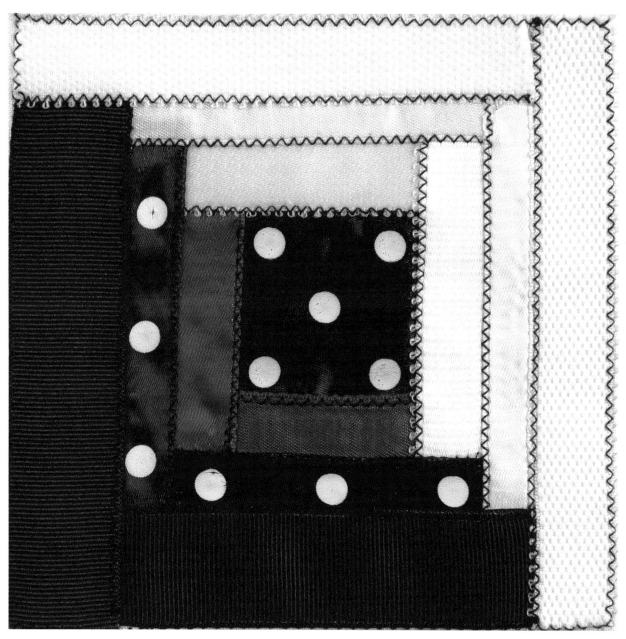

Lengths of ribbon are machine-stitched with narrow zigzag to a background fabric

INSERTED EMBELLISHMENTS

For added texture and interest, a number of different textural elements can be inserted in the seams of Log Cabin blocks. These include piping, frills, lace and broderie anglaise edgings, fringes or frayed strips, tiny tabs, rouleaux loops and prairie points. In each case the embellishment is tacked face up on the previous strip with the raw edges aligned, then the next strip of fabric is stitched through all three layers so that the embellishment hangs free.

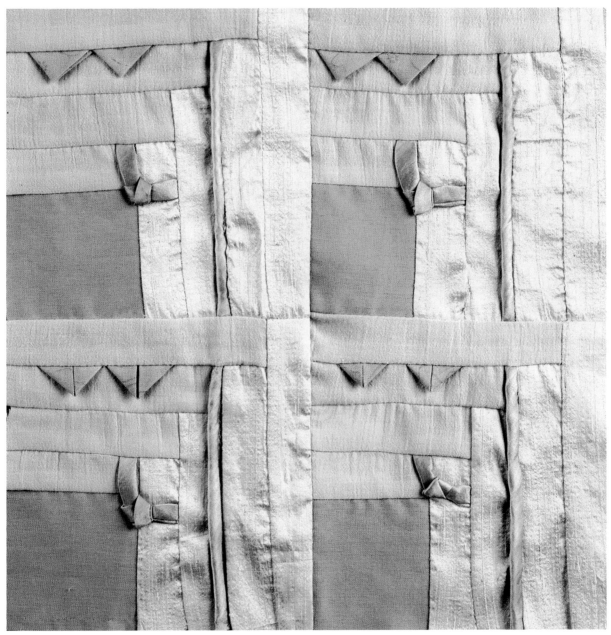

Four asymmetric blocks are decorated with knotted rouleaux, prairie points and piping

Rouleaux

Rouleaux are tubes of fabric which can be formed into loops, spirals or knots. They can be used singly or in overlapping groups. It is essential to use fine fabric such as poplin, lawn, or silk, as turning the tube through to the right side can be difficult with rough-surfaced fabric.

1 Cut a bias strip of fabric 2.5 (1in) wide.

2 Fold in half lengthwise with right sides together.

3 Machine-stitch 6mm (¼in) from the folded edge, leaving the ends open and

the seam allowance untrimmed as this will act as a filling for the rouleau.

4 Attach a length of strong cotton to one end of the tube. Thread the cotton on a large needle or bodkin and insert it eye-first through the tube. Pull gently, so that the tube is gradually pulled through, and finishes with the right side outermost.

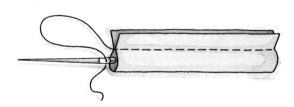

Inserting needle to turn the rouleau

5 Form the rouleau into individual, or continuous, loops or knots and then tack in place.

Prairie Points

There are two methods of folding squares into triangular shapes for inserting into seams. Choose a fabric such as cotton which can be crisply pressed.

1 Cut a number of 5cm (2in) squares of fabric.

2 Fold each square in half to form a rectangle and press firmly. Bring the corners of the folded edge to meet at the centre of the opposite side. Press well.

3 These can then be stitched in place for inserting into a seam and can be used with either side uppermost, overlapped, or used singly.

Folding the squares for the first Prairie Point method

The second method can be used in a similar way to the first, or interleaved as follows.

1 Cut a number of 5cm (2in) squares of fabric.

2 Fold in half diagonally and press well.

3 Fold in half diagonally again, to form a triangle.

4 Slip the folded side of each triangle into the open side of the preceding one and tack them in place, ready for inserting into the seam.

 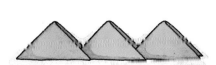

Folding and assembling the Prairie Points for the second method

OPTICAL EFFECTS

The very essence of successful Log Cabin design is the effect of different colours and fabrics juxtaposed or used in opposition to each other. The visual impact of these hues and tones makes the technique one of the most interesting patchwork methods. To take this a stage further, various optical effects can be created by the clever use of tonal value and colour. 'Op' art was popularized in the 1960s by artists such as Victor Vasarely and Bridget Riley, but the idea of creating optical illusions goes back several hundred years. Some of the most familiar patchwork designs, such as Tumbling (or Baby's) Blocks rely for their effect on carefully selected tones. These can be adapted or modified using Log Cabin blocks of various shapes.

Tumbling Blocks is made up of three diamond-shaped blocks – one dark-toned, one medium-toned and one light-toned in hue. These are juxtaposed to create a three-dimensional stepped design. In addition, the strips can be graduated in tone within the Log Cabin block to give even greater effect.

A tumbling blocks design made up with one of the diamonds edged with narrow Log Cabin strips

A development of this idea can be made with units of two diamonds and a square, or a long diamond and two parallelograms, each with carefully selected tones.

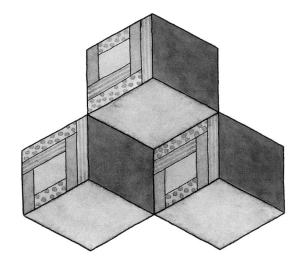

Tumbling Blocks reflected vertically

Tumbling Blocks

A pattern which works in a similar three-dimensional way is an adaptation of the block known as Attic Windows, which has a large square with strips of different tones on two sides. This block can also be set on point to produce a trellis effect.

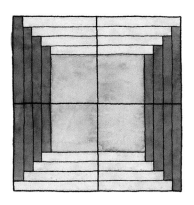

Four reflected blocks

Attic Windows

Four reflected blocks

Four identical blocks on point

The choice of fabric can also give the visual effect great impact. Interesting designs can be developed with striped fabrics, carefully cut with the stripes spiralling around a block and creating movement around the shape. A different effect will be made if the stripes run across the strips. Careful matching is essential for a formal design, whereas cutting the stripes randomly can look spontaneous.

Shot fabrics – usually of silk, or shiny synthetic fabrics – present interesting possibilities, as they are woven with the warp in one colour and the weft in another. With the Log Cabin strips stitched at right-angles to one another, the light falling on them will show up the different colours and produce an iridescent three-dimensional effect.

PICTORIAL EFFECTS

This method has been explored by a number of textile artists in the United States, including Flavin Glover, who is well-known for her quilts depicting landscapes and townscapes (see opposite). Pictorial Log Cabin lends itself to large-scale works such as wallhangings or quilts, with the blocks pieced in the traditional concentric way or using the Courthouse Steps method. If you decide to embark on this technique you should draft the design on squared paper, colouring in the blocks with the appropriate colours. For well-defined shapes or images, blocks with a large number of narrow strips are most suitable, and some blocks will need to be constructed entirely of one fabric or closely related fabrics to achieve the background.

Pointed shapes, such as roofs or hills, can be effectively created using Courthouse Steps blocks, Rose Pattern blocks can depict flowers of various types and circular Log Cabin can

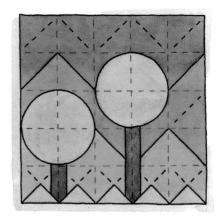

Drafting a 25 block picture with a combination of circular, Courthouse Steps and traditional blocks

Chasing the Wind *by Flavin Glover. Machine-pieced basic blocks, hand quilted cotton and cotton-blend fabrics*

portray the sun, balls, balloons, flowers or round trees. Detached, semi-detached, or terraced houses can be created with square or rectangular blocks, and the centre patches of these can form windows. These blocks are also good for skyscrapers or office blocks. Still-life

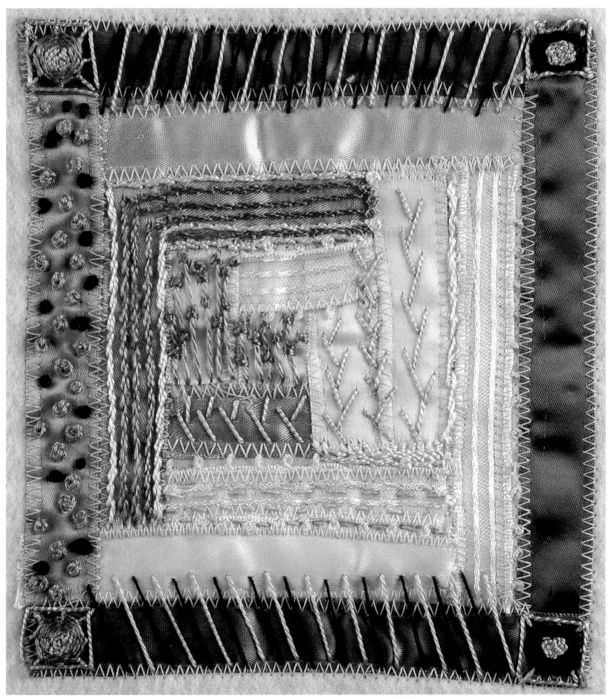

Ribbon Log Cabin enhanced with embroidery stitches, by Anna Griffiths

subjects may present more of a challenge, but fruit and flowers are possibilities using circular and rose pattern techniques.

Details on pictorial quilts can be superimposed by using appliqué shapes or embroidery stitches, depending on the scale.

COMBINING LOG CABIN WITH OTHER TEXTILE TECHNIQUES

A favourite way of experimenting with different types of patchwork is to make a sampler quilt. This involves stitching a group of similar-sized blocks in different techniques and piecing them together with a sashing (or lattice) of plain coordinating fabric between them. It is wise to make the blocks from fabrics of similar pattern and colour, to achieve a satisfactory harmonious effect. You should also check the fibre content of all the fabrics if the item is to be laundered. This idea can be further explored by using only Log Cabin techniques and variations.

Piecing a selection of blocks of different techniques together without sashing can be more challenging and the design needs to be drafted to ensure a good result. Courthouse Steps blocks can be satisfactorily alternated with Nine-patch Star blocks such as 'Shoo-fly' or 'Texas Star' to give the effect of an all-over design on point.

An alternative is to make a background of a Log Cabin block or blocks and add a complementary appliqué design on top. For this the colours and tones should be carefully chosen so that the Log Cabin does not overpower the appliqué.

USING LOG CABIN AS A FRAME

Log Cabin can be used as a fabric frame to surround and enhance a wide variety of

Four tie-dyed rectangles are framed with Log Cabin strips to make a larger rectangle

patchwork techniques when making up single blocks, quilts, throws, cushions and wallhangings. Simply add the required number of strips around the article to be framed, treating the patchwork as the centre patch. You can use either the basic construction or the Courthouse Steps method.

It can also be an ideal way of framing other textile techniques, such as hand- or machine-embroidered panels, quilting, beading, counted thread and needlepoint tapestry. Choose fabrics which complement the main work, such as cotton with quilting, silk with beading, or woollen fabric with needlepoint, and use this to surround the centrepiece with the appropriate strips. A set of embroidered cushions could have Log Cabin frames made in the same fabric as your curtains; an appliqué quilt or wallhanging could be framed with coordinating fabrics, or a beaded evening bag finished with a few rows of Log Cabin, with inserted embellishments such as piping or frills.

FINISHING AND MAKING UP

The need for the thoughtful presentation and finishing of a patchwork project should not be underestimated. Most articles will benefit from a carefully selected and beautifully executed trimming in appropriate materials. Indeed, a humble cushion or ordinary quilt can be greatly enhanced by being well finished, whereas an otherwise satisfactory article may be ruined by using unsympathetic bindings or frills.

Patchwork is often associated with quilting and the Log Cabin technique is no exception. A layer of wadding, together with a lining or backing, will add both weight and warmth to an item, as well as giving an extra textural or decorative dimension. Embroidery stitches by hand or machine can also be added together with appliqué motifs.

It is best to choose a border or binding at the outset, so that it complements the piece both

Left: detail of Hannelore Braunsberg's **The Seasons**

in colour and scale. Select fabrics which harmonize or tone with the patchwork and look carefully at the proportions of the trimming in relation to the whole. An over-wide frill in a garish colour may overshadow a delicate piece, or a very pale, narrow binding may look mean and insignificant on a large, boldly patterned quilt.

QUILTING

Quilting is suitable for a large number of projects including quilts, throws, cushions and wallhangings, as well as waistcoats, jackets and smaller padded accessories such as bags. In the majority of cases this is best done when the patchwork has been completed, though the Quilt-as-you-go method (see page 66) is a good way of padding small single blocks for table mats or cushions.

Wadded (or English) quilting is the most usual way of padding a patchwork article.

Contour quilting in thick thread makes a decorative impact on the design

It consists of three layers – the patchwork top, a layer of wadding and a backing or lining. These are tacked together and stitched by hand or machine in straight lines, simple designs, or more intricate patterns. The choice of wadding depends on the effect you wish to create and the use of the project (see page 11). The quilting stitches can be worked in an unobtrusive way, so that they simply serve to hold the layers together. In this case the most usual method is to stitch by hand or machine along the line of the seams of the blocks or strips, known as 'stitching in the ditch', as the stitching is almost invisible. An alternative is contour (or echo) quilting, where the lines of stitches are worked about 6mm (¼in) either side, or on one side, of some of the seam lines.

Machine stitching can also be used – either free-machining over part or all of the patchwork (see page 87), or an automatic embroidery stitch along the lines of the design. The advantage of all these methods of quilting is that there is no need to mark the design on the fabric.

TACKING

For successful hand or machine quilting it is essential that the three layers are tacked firmly together. Do not be tempted to neglect this important stage, as failing to secure the layers will mean that they will move during the quilting process, distorting the final shape. You can now buy tacking guns to hold the layers together with plastic staples but, although these can make a quick alternative to tacking by hand, particularly for large-scale projects, they should not be used on fine fabrics such as silk or satin, as the staples may leave holes.

Usually the layers are tacked together before framing, although there are instances where the backing fabric is framed separately.

1 Place the wadding on top of the backing fabric, and then the patchwork on top of that, right side uppermost, so that the wadding is sandwiched between the two layers. Check that the grain lines of the patchwork and the backing are aligned. Pin the layers together with plenty of long, glass-headed pins, smoothing out any wrinkles from the centre, so that the finished shape is retained.

2 Thread a long needle with ordinary sewing cotton and, starting in the centre, work a row of large tacking stitches about 5cm (2in) in length to the lower edge, and then another row to the top edge. Follow this with a similar horizontal row across the centre. Working outwards in a systematic fashion, make rows of tacking stitches about 7.5cm (3in) apart, in grid formation, until the surface is entirely covered.

Tacking with the backing fabric framed

If you are using a large quilting frame or a tapestry frame, it is preferable to attach the backing fabric to the frame before tacking the wadding and patchwork top. With decorative panels or small items, where the effect of plenty of loft is required, stretching all three

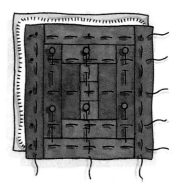

Tacking ready for quilting

layers in a frame would flatten the wadding. In these cases, frame up the backing fabric in the usual way. Place the wadding and the patchwork loosely on top and tack as above, smoothing out any wrinkles as you go.

FRAMING

Although small projects can be hand quilted with the work unframed, in most cases it is preferable to mount the prepared fabrics in a frame. This will enable you to retain the correct tension of stitching and the work will remain free from distortion and need no ironing.

When mounting work in a frame make sure that the warp and weft of the fabrics run at right-angles to one another.

Quilting Hoops

These wooden hoops, similar but more robust than embroidery hoops, have an outer ring which is adjustable with a

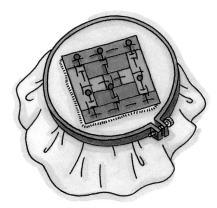

Assembling a quilting hoop

screw (see facing page). They are suitable for small projects especially if the whole design will fit within the bounds of the frame. If you need to relocate the frame to another part of the design, make sure that you do not crease or damage previously stitched areas. Always remove the work from the frame when you have finished a quilting session, otherwise the imprint of the frame may spoil the end result.

1 Loosen the screw of the outer hoop, place the prepared fabric over the inner hoop, then press the outer hoop down over the quilting and the inner hoop.

2 Make sure the grain of the fabric is straight. Tighten the screw to hold the quilting firmly – but not too tautly – in place.

Tubular Clip Frames

These are available in a range of sizes, including those large enough for a quilt or throw. They consist of four tubular components which join up to make a rectangle; the fabric is laid over the frame with the outer tubes clamping it in place. Because of the rectangular form, there is less chance of the work being stretched on the bias, than when using a circular or oval hoop.

Quilting frames

Traditional quilting frames large enough to accommodate a full-scale quilt are only

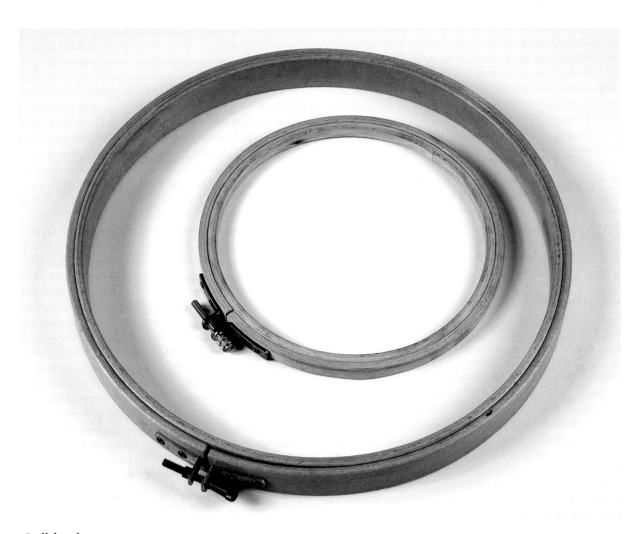

Quilting hoops

a worthwhile investment if you have plenty of space and are planning to make a number of major projects. Tapestry (or slate) frames, which are used by embroiderers, are similar but smaller in scale and are suitable for small household furnishings such as cushions, or sections of garments and accessories. When using either of these frames, the backing fabric is usually framed up and the wadding and patchwork tacked on afterwards. Floor stands, which allow you to have both hands free for stitching are available for both types.

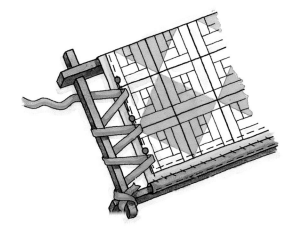

Assembling a traditional quilting frame

1 Mark the centre of the webbing attached to the rollers, and make a corresponding mark at the centre top and bottom of the backing fabric. Fold a narrow hem along the top edge of the fabric. Pin this folded edge along the webbing, aligning the centre marks, and overcast the two together with strong thread, starting in the centre and working outwards. Repeat with the bottom edge on the other roller.

2 Roll any excess length of backing fabric onto the bottom roller, then insert the side stretchers and secure them with split pins or pegs, so that the fabric is evenly tensioned but not too taut.

3 Tension the sides of the fabric with lengths of tape. Tie one end of the tape to the stretcher and start pinning to the edge of the backing fabric. Take the tape over the side stretcher diagonally and pin again on the edge of the backing. Continue along the length of the stretcher, pulling the tape evenly, and tie off at the other end. Repeat with a second piece of tape along the other edge.

STITCHING

Choose a sewing cotton, or thicker quilting thread, which contrasts or tones with the predominant colours of the patchwork.

If you are quilting a project such as a quilt or a reversible garment, which needs to look as good on the back as on the front, it is important to start and finish the stitching as unobtrusively as possible.

Starting to Stitch

Thread the needle with about 45cm (18in) thread and make a small knot a short distance from the end. Bring the needle up through the three layers to the patchwork top. Tug gently so that the knot pulls through the backing fabric and into the wadding, then start stitching.

If the look of the back is of little importance, such as on a cushion, you can start with a double backstitch or a small knot on the backing fabric.

Stitching

Most patchwork projects are quilted with small evenly spaced running stitches with a consistent tension. This evenness is in fact more crucial than the actual size of the stitches. Start in the centre of the piece and gradually work outwards, completing each section before moving onto the next. With a little practice you will achieve a rhythm which will result in a perfect row of stitching.

For large projects it is best to use a thimble – if you are right-handed, on the middle finger of the right hand. Another thimble can be used underneath the work on the first finger of the left hand.

Working from right to left (or left to right if you are left-handed) bring the needle in and out of the layers of fabric, making small

evenly spaced stitches. Whether you can pick up two or three stitches before pulling the needle through will depend on the thickness of the wadding. The underneath hand will guide the needle, and the thimble on the top hand can push it through.

Finishing

To finish off the stitching invisibly, take the thread through the wadding a short way, bring it out through the backing fabric and cut off the thread close to the surface. For other methods, finish with a double backstitch in the backing fabric.

MACHINE QUILTING

Although hand quilting can be a restful form of recreation and its appearance is a traditional feature, using a sewing machine will speed up the process and if done with care does not have to compromise the quality of the finished piece. Sewing machines all have a variety of attachments so you should refer to your handbook for any special instructions. It is essential to get to know your sewing machine thoroughly before embarking on a project.

Conventional Machine Stitching

As with hand quilting, take care with the preparation and tacking-up to ensure that the work retains its shape and does not distort despite not being mounted in a frame. For overall designs, try to stitch in the same direction, from top to bottom, starting at the centre top and working towards the sides. For more complex designs start in the centre and work outwards. When stitching diagonally you will need to be especially careful that you do not pull the patchwork out of its rectangular shape along the bias.

It is usual to machine-quilt patchworked designs using a long stitch. You can purchase a walking foot as an extra accessory which will ride over the thickness of the wadding. If you are using a regular sewing foot you may need to ease the fabric slightly under the needle. When quilting 'in the ditch' (see page 82) make sure the needle pierces the patchwork seam or, if you prefer to work contour quilting (see page 82), use the width of the machine foot to guide you or alter the needle position accordingly.

If you are working an automatic embroidery stitch across or along the lines of the patchwork, stitch a practice piece first to determine the effect, not only of the stitch, but also of your choice of colour.

Free-machining

This can be an effective way of flattening areas of wadding so that certain aspects of the design are emphasized in relief. The feed dogs of the machine are disengaged to a 'darning' position so that the fabric can be moved in any direction beneath the foot. It is essential that you practise this technique until you are proficient as it is difficult and tedious to unpick mistakes.

1 Disengage the feed dogs of the machine and set the stitch width and length to 0. Remove the regular presser foot and substitute a darning foot.

2 Lower the presser bar and bring both threads to the surface of the patchwork. Insert the needle and start stitching, moving the fabric in such a way that you are drawing with the needle.

3 One of the most useful free-style stitches is known as 'vermicelli'. To work this, stitch a series of tiny loops and curves to completely cover the surface of the area to be quilted.

Free-style machine quilting in vermicelli stitch flattens some areas of the design

MAKING UP WALLHANGINGS AND SOFT FURNISHINGS

If a throw or wallhanging has been quilted, the best way is to bind the edge with a toning fabric as the backing of the quilting will act as a satisfactory lining. For patchwork which has not been quilted, it is necessary to add a lining, or, in the case of cushions, a back made from a fabric which complements the design. Additional decoration can be added in the form of piping or frills, which can also enhance garments, accessories and soft furnishing items.

Binding and Piping

Although you can buy ready-made bias bindings, these are usually of thin fabric and are intended as finishings for the inside of dressmaking projects. If you cut your own binding, it can be made in exactly the type of fabric you require, and in a colour which will enhance the project. Likewise you can choose the thickness of the piping cord which best suits the scale of the cushion, quilt or accessory. Small rectangular or square items made with the quilt-as-you-go method can be trimmed with straight strip binding, whilst those with curved edges will need to be edged with bias binding.

Straight Strip Binding

Although bias binding is the best option for articles with curved or complicated outlines,

A silk bag in Round the Houses pattern is trimmed with piping, binding and a plaited rouleau handle

straight strip binding is suitable for rectangular quilts, throws and wall-hangings. Decide on the width by doubling the finished width and adding two seam allowances. Long lengths will need to be joined on the straight grain and the binding on the vertical sides of the article should be completed before binding the other two edges.

1 With right sides together, align the raw edges of the binding and the article. Pin, tack and stitch along the stitching line.

2 Fold the binding in half lengthwise and turn under the raw edge. Pin and tack this folded edge to align with the stitching on the wrong side of the work.

3 Slipstitch in place, folding in the ends to complete a neat corner.

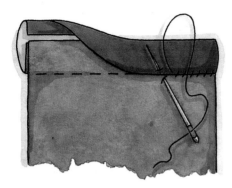

Attaching a bias or straight strip binding

Bias Binding

This binding is essential for articles which have curved edges, as the bias-cut strip will stretch sufficiently to accommodate both concave and convex corners.

The width is determined in a similar way to that of straight stitch binding (see previous page) but is cut diagonally across the fabric at a 45° angle to the edge. The simplest way to establish this is to use the diagonal line on your cutting mat. Long lengths should be joined on the straight grain.

Stitch and fold as for straight strip binding, clipping the curves and into any inward corners. Allow extra binding to accommodate outside corners, easing the binding to fit. Fold the binding in half lengthwise, and finish by turning the edge and slipstitching as for straight strip binding.

Double Binding

For a firmer, more substantial binding for large-scale projects such as quilts and throws, you can make a double binding. To calculate the width of the straight or bias strip, multiply the width of the finished binding by four and add two seam allowances. Long lengths will need to be joined as for normal binding.

1 Fold the binding in half lengthwise with wrong sides together. Align the two raw

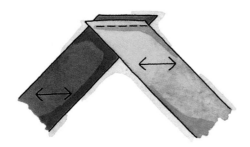

Attaching a bias strip

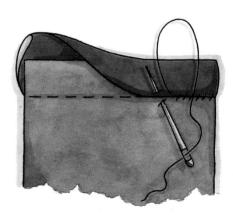

Attaching a double binding

edges of the binding and that on the right side of the article. Pin, tack and stitch along the stitching line as for normal binding.

2 Fold the binding in half lengthwise to the back of the work and then slipstitch the fold down to the wrong side of the stitching.

Piping

Piping makes a good finish for cushions, bags and garments and is inserted in a seam as a raised fabric-covered cord. Piping cord is available in several thicknesses, so you can chose one which is appropriate in scale both to the fabric and to the size of the article. Although some types of piping cord are pre-shrunk, it is still advisable to wash it in boiling water and dry before use.

Joining and stitching piping to a block

1 Cut and, if necessary, stitch a lengthwise join for a bias strip twice the width of the piping cord, plus two seam allowances.

With the right sides out, fold the bias strip over the piping cord with the raw edges together.

2 Attach a zipper foot to the machine. Tack and machine-stitch to hold. Leave the ends unstitched for joining later.

3 With raw edges aligned, pin, tack and machine-stitch the piping to the right side of the article, clipping curves or inward corners.

4 If necessary join the bias fabric on the straight grain to fit the article (for example around the perimeter of a cushion). Cut and abut the ends of the piping cord. Fold over the bias strip and stitch in place.

5 Add the lining (or the back of the cushion) and turn the work to the right side.

Frills

Frills make a pretty, decorative edging for trimming cushions, cot quilts, small accessories and soft furnishing items. They are usually inserted into the seam between the front and back, or lining of a project.

The depth of the frill should be assessed in conjunction with the scale of the project and the thickness of the fabric. Narrow gathered frills are best made from doubled fabric, while pleated frills present a stylish and contemporary approach.

Gathered frills

A single frill has the free edge hemmed by hand or machine, while for a double frill the fabric is folded in half lengthwise. For a single frill, the width is determined by assessing the finished depth and adding the seam and hem allowances. Cut a straight strip to this depth and between one and a half times and twice the length of the edge that will be trimmed.

1 For a continuous frill around a quilt or cushion, join the two ends and make a hem along one edge, either by hand or machine. Work two parallel lines of gathering stitches 6mm (1/4in) from the raw edge.

2 Divide the length of the frill into four equal sections and mark at four points. Mark the edge to be trimmed at four equidistant places.

3 Pull up the gathering threads evenly, so that each section coincides with the marks on the edge of the article to be trimmed. With right sides and raw edges together, pin and tack the frill in place, distributing the gathers evenly and allowing extra fullness at any corners.

4 Add the lining or backing and turn the work to the right side.

5 For a double frill, decide on the finished depth, then double this measurement and add seam allowances. Fold the fabric in half lengthwise, gather through both layers of fabric and proceed as for a single frill.

Pleated frills

Cut and prepare the strip of fabric, either single or double, as for gathered frills, allowing at least three times the length to accommodate the pleats. Pin and tack the strip into carefully measured pleats. Stitch to the article as for a gathered frill.

MAKING UP

Lining and Interlining Wallhangings

Log cabin wallhangings which have not been quilted with a binding around the edge need to have a lining and maybe an interlining attached. Both these should be chosen in relation to the scale and weight

Attaching a single frill

Metamorphosis: *a silk hanging using a combination of quilting, frayed-edge Log Cabin and freestanding appliqué leaves is suspended on a perspex rod with loops*

of the hanging. Interlinings are available in a number of different weights and fibres. Very large-scale works require heavyweight woven interlinings, such as tailor's canvas or sailcloth, while a non-woven interfacing will suffice for smaller projects. For the lining, choose a curtain lining or similar fabric.

1 Cut the interlining to the size of the finished hanging, and tack it in place on the back of the work.

2 Fold the two sides of the hanging over the interlining and secure in place with herringbone stitch. Complete the top and lower hem in the same way. For extra weight, which will ensure that the finished work hangs straight, you can stitch small curtain weights at intervals inside the lower hem.

Attaching an interlining before lining

3 Cut the lining on the straight grain, making it slightly larger than the finished patchwork. Turn under and press the edges, adding the sleeve or Velcro strip, if desired. Pin, tack and slipstitch the lining to the back of the work, incorporating the tabs if that is your chosen method of hanging. The bottom edge can either be stitched as for the other three sides, or a hem can be made which is left to hang free.

HANGING METHODS

Log Cabin is an ideal technique for creating wallhangings and you should decide on the method of hanging when you work out the original design. You can stitch a series of tabs or loops to the top edge and insert a brass pole, Perspex rod or wooden dowel. If you propose to exhibit your project, you will find that most quilt shows require a sleeve to be attached to the back. Alternatively Velcro can be attached to the quilt or hanging and the other Velcro strip stapled or glued to a wooden batten which is screwed to the wall.

Tabs
These can vary in length and width, depending on the scale of the work, but there should be a sufficient number placed at regular intervals for the wallhanging to hang smoothly.

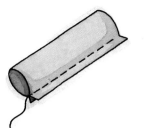

Preparing tabs

1 For each tab cut a strip double the finished width, plus a 2.5cm (1in) seam allowance.

2 Fold in half lengthwise with right sides together and stitch along the length. Turn the tube to the right side and press with the seam running down the centre back.

3 Fold in half and attach firmly to the back of the hanging, tucking under the raw edges.

Sleeves

A sleeve is a narrow strip of fabric, attached to the top edge of the back of a quilt or wallhanging, through which a rod or batten is inserted.

1 Cut a 10cm (4in) strip of fabric the same length as the top of the wallhanging. Press and stitch a small hem at either end and then press a 12mm (½in) hem along both edges.

2 Pin, tack and stitch this firmly by hand to the back of the hanging, roughly 2.5cm (1in) from the top edge. Make sure the stitches go through the wadding, if the hanging is quilted, but do not show on the front.

3 Insert a wooden lath or aluminium strip, stitch up the ends of the sleeve and add a curtain ring at either end from which to hang the piece.

Attaching a sleeve and rings

CUSHIONS

Although there are a number of ways of making up cushions, the simplest is to add a back to the cushion front, insert a zip or simply slipstitch the opening. The trimming such as piping or frill should be attached to the cushion front with the raw edges aligned and the trimming facing inwards.

A cushion with painted and quilted central square and Flying Geese pattern border is completed with matching piping

1 Cut the back exactly the same size as the front. With right sides together, pin, tack and stitch by hand or machine, around the perimeter, through all layers, leaving a long gap along one side.

2 Turn the work through to the right side, insert the cushion pad, and stitch up the gap.

3 If you are inserting a zip, start by stitching one side of the assembled cushion front and back, leaving a gap for the zip. Turn to the right side and insert the zip in the gap. Open the zip and complete the other three sides. Continue as above.

GALLERY

Today the craft of Log Cabin patchwork is being reassessed continually. Textile artists are experimenting with the craft, and finding ways to bring a contemporary approach to this age-old technique. The use of unconventional materials and finishes is bringing excitement and individuality to the basic method, and revitalizing the original designs and patterns.

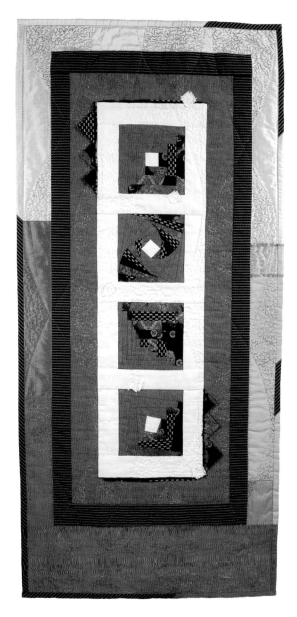

Sugar and Spice by Nikki Tinkler
Originally four teaching samples using a mixture of oriental and western fabrics. Hand quilted with areas of seeding with hand-dyed threads

Log Cabin Jewels: *silk panel with frayed fabric, Prairie Points and piping*

Two cushions in the basic Log Cabin construction. *The one on the left uses printed furnishing fabrics, whilst the one on the right is made up of dress-weight corduroys*

Log Cabin Throw: *36 identical blocks of basic Log Cabin construction are joined to form a chequered pattern with diagonal quilting*

A Log Cabin table mat *is further embellished with an appliqué motif*

Two cushions in pastel colours: *on the left a Round the Houses pattern surrounds a quilted centre, on the right a diamond-effect centre with Prairie Point embellishment*

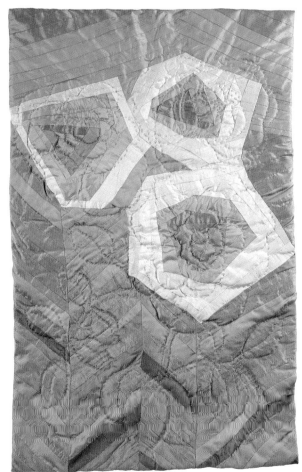

Roses, Roses all the Way: *rose pattern Log Cabin hanging in silk with hand quilting*

Tweed Bag *by Janice Lawrence*: *a sophisticated approach to the Courthouse Steps method using a selection of woollen fabrics*

Floral Triangles: *six triangular Log Cabin blocks made from furnishing fabric samples to make a hanging*

Evening bag:
*panne velvet strips
and cord make a
finishing touch for
this embroidered
satin design*

**Purse with
piped edge and
covered button**:
*pure silk fabrics in a
variation of
Pineapple Pattern
Log Cabin.*

**Three ribbon
pincushions** *using
different machine
stitching*

Triangle Bag:
*marbled fabric and
plain cottons make
a striking effect*

Bag: *a Flying Geese design with large central square makes an attractive bag for holidays or everyday use*

Diamonds are Forever: *asymmetric blocks have been placed on point, to form a diamond-effect hanging*

Persian Doorway: *this hanging was inspired by the design of the furnishing fabric. The Courthouse Steps variation leads the eye to the central square.*

Spring, *from* **The Seasons**, *by Hannelore Braunsberg*
(Photographed by Suzanne Grundy)

Summer, *from* **The Seasons**, *by Hannelore Braunsberg*
(Photographed by Suzanne Grundy)

Autumn, *from* **The Seasons***, by Hannelore Braunsberg*
(Photographed by Suzanne Grundy)

Winter, *from* **The Seasons**, *by Hannelore Braunsberg*
(Photographed by Suzanne Grundy).

ABOUT THE AUTHOR

Pauline Brown is a well-known textile artist and she brings her expertise and experience as a teacher of patchwork and quilting, as well as of embroidery and design, to her written work. She is the author of a number of well-received books on embroidery, appliqué and patchwork, including *The Creative Quilter*, *Patchwork for Beginners* and *Decoration on Fabric*, also published by GMC Publications.

Pauline has exhibited widely throughout the United Kingdom and her work is in many private collections. In addition, she has been commissioned to produce work for a number of places of worship, as well as for corporate venues.

INDEX

TITLES AVAILABLE FROM
GMC Publications

BOOKS

MAGAZINES

WOODTURNING ◆ WOODCARVING
FURNITURE & CABINETMAKING
THE ROUTER ◆ NEW WOODWORKING
THE DOLLS' HOUSE MAGAZINE
OUTDOOR PHOTOGRAPHY
BLACK & WHITE PHOTOGRAPHY
TRAVEL PHOTOGRAPHY
MACHINE KNITTING NEWS
GUILD OF MASTER CRAFTSMEN NEWS

The above represents a selection of the titles currently published or scheduled to be published.
All are available direct from the Publishers or through bookshops, newsagents and specialist retailers.
To place an order, or to obtain a complete catalogue, contact:

**GMC Publications,
Castle Place, 166 High Street, Lewes,
East Sussex BN7 1XU United Kingdom
Tel: 01273 488005 Fax: 01273 402866
E-mail: pubs@thegmcgroup.com**

Orders by credit card are accepted